The Impact of Outages on Prices and Investment in the US Oil Refining Industry

June 12, 2014

Abstract

This paper considers the effects of refinery outages (due to planned turn-arounds or unplanned events) on current petroleum product prices and future refinery investment. Empirical evidence on these relationships is mixed and highly dependent on the size and duration of the outage, the geographic area considered, the level of inventories available at the time of the outage, and the tightness of the market as measured by the capacity utilization rate. Using a detailed database of plant-level refinery outages for both upstream and downstream refining units, I estimate the effects of outages on product prices controlling for the crude oil price and the ability of operating plants to respond to the outage. I also consider the effect of current market profitability on the likelihood of planned refinery outages and the effects of high utilization rates and planned maintenance on the prospects for unplanned outages. I then use plant-level capacity data to analyze the effects of outages, profitability, and utilization rates on future investment decisions of the refinery.

Results based on OLS and probit models show that planned outages tend to occur during the spring and fall and during times of relatively low margins as measured by the crack spread. The length of time since the last plant turn-around is positively associated with future unplanned outages. Price regressions show that atmospheric distillation and catalytic cracking outages are positively associated with gasoline prices and the association is stronger the higher is the utilization rate at the time of the outage. The relationship between both upstream and downstream investment and outages is mixed though refiners tend to invest less when nearby plants have made investments in the prior year. While causal relationships between outages, prices, and investment are difficult to estimate due to simultaneity and unobserved variables, these descriptive results show that outages are an important factor affecting refined product prices and future refinery investment.

---

*Email: mchesnes@ftc.gov. Web: http://www.chesnes.com. I thank John Rust, Ginger Jin and Peter Cramton for their support. I am also grateful to Louis Silvia, Chris Taylor, Nick Kreisle, David Meyer, David Schmidt, Daniel Hosken, Ted Rosenbaum and seminar participants at the Federal Trade Commission, the University of Maryland, the Federal Reserve Board of Governors, and La Pietra-Mondragone Workshop in Economics for their suggestions and comments. All remaining errors are my own. The opinions expressed here are those of the author and not necessarily those of the Federal Trade Commission or any of its Commissioners.

is little excess capacity. Therefore, I next focus on unplanned outages. While weather events can occur randomly and affect a large number of plants, other idiosyncratic outages that only affect one plant (such as a refinery fire) may be related to the utilization rate at which the plant is running or the time since the plant last performed a turn-around.[5]

Once I understand when and why outages occur, I then focus on the effect of the outages on product prices. Some studies (EIA, (2011)) have found very little correlation between outages and product prices with crude oil price fluctuations being the primary driver of the variation in product prices. One benefit of the detailed outage data that I employ is that outages are reported by refining unit. Since some units (such as the Fluid Catalytic Cracking or FCC unit) are more important for the production of certain products (such as gasoline), I can determine how certain types of outages affect different product prices. Outages that occur during periods of low demand or high inventories likely have less of a price effect compared to periods where inventories are relatively low and/or utilization rates are high because plants are less able to respond to nearby outages. Therefore, my analysis will control for the level of market tightness at the time of the outage when assessing its impact.

Finally, I consider the effects of outages, price spreads, and utilization rates on investment decisions of the refiners. I expect that unplanned outages during a given year might lead to future investment as a refiner wants to update their plant and avoid future outages. In years following relatively wide crack spreads, one might expect more investment if refiners expect that profitability will remain favorable in the future. However, since the crack spread is highly variable, it may serve as a poor predictor of future investment. Investments in capacity may also be larger if a plant found it optimal to run at a high utilization rate in the prior year. If high utilization rates generally lead to more unplanned outages, then investing in more capacity can help avoid future outages.[6] My data allow me to study investments in both upstream (atmospheric distillation) capacity and in downstream units. This is important because refiners may find it optimal to increase the complexity of their plant by investing in downstream units such as hydrocrackers and reformers that allow them more flexibility in their crude oil or production slates.

While a fully structural model of the refining industry may provide important insights into the industry and how it responds to shocks, the complexity of the input and output choices, the heterogeneous technology, and other factors make modeling this behavior intractable.[7] The reduced-form approach in this paper allows to me assess the relationships between key variables and gain insights into how the oil refining industry responds to shocks, while averaging over some of the variation not captured by the model (such a refiner's choice of different types of crude oil). There are likely unobserved variables that affect product prices, outages, and refiners' investment decisions. In addition, it is possible that there are simultaneity issues (for example, between planned outages and product prices) that make conclusions about causality difficult. Therefore, while these results are descriptive, they show that outages are an important factor in determining

---

[5] Unfortunately, I do not observe plant-level utilization rates, but I do observe utilization rates at the refining district level. However, even these utilization rates only reflect the rate of atmospheric distillation (the first phase of refining) and not the production intensity of downstream units.

[6] I also consider how product inventories and investments by competing plants may affect future investment decisions.

[7] In technical terms, the state space of crude and product prices, capacities, and inventories (to name a few) is very large. Modeling only a subset of these state variables masks important variation that is important to the refiner as he optimizes production each period.

refined product prices and future refinery investment.

Plants need to perform regular maintenance each year no matter how high their margins so some plants still perform planned turn-arounds even during periods of high crack spreads. However, my results indicate that planned outages tend to occur more often during the spring and fall when demand for gasoline is generally lower and during times of relatively low margins as measured by the crack spread. The length of time since the last plant turn-around is positively associated with future unplanned outages. Unplanned outages are actually negatively associated with the utilization rate, though utilization is only available at the PADD[8] level and is therefore a imprecise measure of the impact of plant-level production intensity on unplanned outages.[9]

Price regressions show that atmospheric distillation and catalytic cracking outages have positive effects on gasoline prices and these effects are larger the higher the utilization rate at the time of the outage. Distillate prices also respond positively to atmospheric distillation outages, but are unaffected by catalytic cracking outages, a unit better-equipped for producing gasoline. Investment in certain refining units is positively associated with planned and unplanned outages of those units, but in general, the relationship between investment and past outages is mixed. Investment in distillation capacity tends to be more likely in a year following relatively high utilization rates and less likely when nearby plants have recently made investments of their own. Refiners may also be responding to unobserved longer-term trends in the operations and profitability of their plants.

The remainder of this paper is organized as follows. In section 2, I provide an overview of the oil refining industry to better understand the complicated problem facing the refiner. I describe my data in section 3 and describe my empirical specifications and results in section 4. Section 5 concludes and provides a discussion of potential extensions.

2   Background on the US Oil Refining Industry

The oil industry is broadly comprised of several vertically oriented segments. They include crude oil exploration and extraction, refineries which convert crude oil into other products, pipeline distribution networks, terminals that store the finished product near major cities, and tanker trucks which transport products to retail outlets.[10] The largest refined product, gasoline, accounts for about 52% of total production, while distillate and jet fuel make up another third.[11] Of the petroleum consumed in the United States, about 70% is used in the transportation sector.[12] Figures 1 and 2 provide a description of the production process and average product yields.[13] The main distillation process produces very little final products like gasoline, but

---

[8]Petroleum Administration for Defense District.

[9]This is also suggestive that refiners are successful at minimizing unplanned outages during periods of high demand (and utilization) by performing planned maintenance in low-demand periods. Further, this result is consistent with the explanation that refiners perform planned maintenance in low-demand (low-utilization) periods and unplanned outages arise during the maintenance.

[10]75% of terminals in the US are owned by independent oil companies and wholesalers and not major oil companies. See US Senate Report (2002), p. 40.

[11]See http://www.eia.gov/dnav/pet/pet_pnp_wprodrb_dcu_nus_4.htm.

[12]See http://www.eia.gov/totalenergy/data/monthly/.

[13]Note the motor gasoline blending components are shown here as a part of refinery production, even though EIA reports them as a (negative) input into refining since they leave the refinery as an unfinished product, later to be mixed with other chemicals

it is complemented by other units that extract more of the highest valued products. Technical details of the refining process and background on the types of crude oil available can be found in the appendix.

Figure 1: Production Process (Source: EIA)

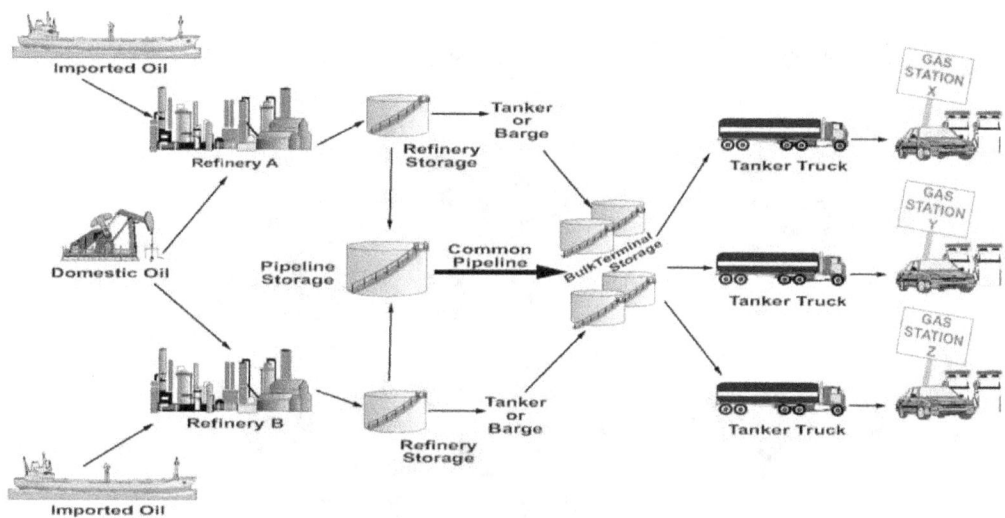

The demand for refined oil products in the US grew steadily during the 1980s and 1990s before peaking at 756 million gallons per day (gpd) 2005. The US consumed 390 million gpd of gasoline in 2007 though consumption fell to 365 million gpd in 2012.[14] Aside from refining crude oil into gasoline, refineries produce many products that are important inputs into other industries. Retail gasoline prices have recently experienced increased variability in the US with prices ranging from $1.09 in 2001 to a high of $4.06 in the summer 2008 before declining to about $3.60 in the summer of 2013. Wholesale prices peaked around $3.40 a gallon in 2008.[15] Many justify the high prices as a result of the growing demand for petroleum products and supply limitations, including the scarcity of crude oil, Middle East uncertainty, hurricanes, and the OPEC cartel. Others claim the high prices result from coordinated anticompetitive behavior by big oil companies or speculation by the financial industry. Outages, investment and utilization choices by oil refineries may also play a significant role in affecting downstream prices.

(usually ethanol) by a blender.

[14] Annual world consumption of crude oil totals 30 billion barrels, of which 7.5 billion barrels is produced in the US. About 60% of crude oil used by refineries is imported and US consumption of refined gasoline represents 40% of world consumption. See http://www.eia.gov/dnav/pet/pet_cons_psup_dc_nus_mbbl_a.htm.

[15] US regular gasoline, source: EIA.

Figure 2: Average Refinery Yields, 2010 (Including Gasoline Blending Components)

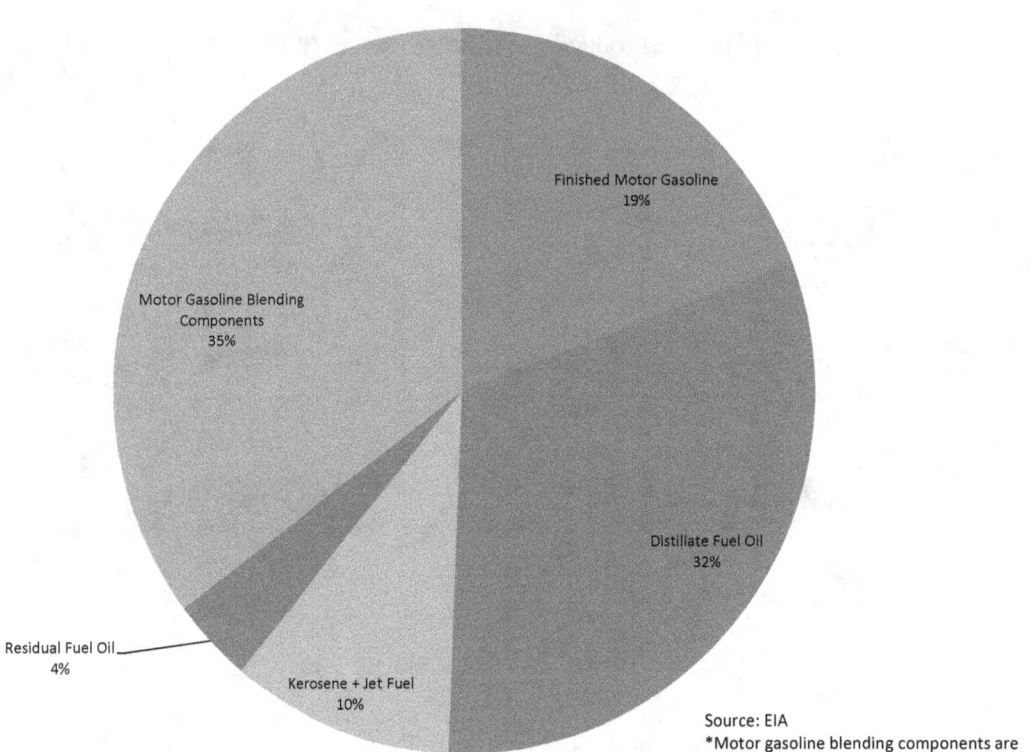

About one-half of US production occurs near the Gulf of Mexico in Texas and Louisiana, though there are significant operations in the Northeast, the Midwest, and California. During World War II, the country was divided into PADDs to aid in the allocation of petroleum products. Figure 3 displays a map of refinery locations along with delineations of the five PADDs.[16]

While some refined products are consumed in areas close to a refinery, an extensive pipeline network transports most refined products to more distant consumption points.[17] Figure 4 shows the major refined products pipelines in the US. With important pipelines connecting the Gulf Coast production center to the population centers in the Northeast and the Midwest, PADDs I, II, and III are closely linked economically. The Rocky Mountain region (PADD IV) is fairly isolated from the rest of the country and imports only limited refined product from other regions. Finally, refiners on the West Coast (PADD V) are also relatively isolated from other refining regions. PADD V also includes California, a state that, due to strict environmental regulations, is limited in its ability to use products that are refined for consumption in other states.

---

[16]PADDs II and III are also subdivided into refining districts.

[17]For instance, the Colonial pipeline, which runs from the Gulf Coast up to the Northeast, was built in 1968. Pipelines now carry 70% of all refined products shipped between PADDs.

Figure 3: US Refineries, PADDs, and Refining Districts

Figure 4: Major Refined Product Pipelines

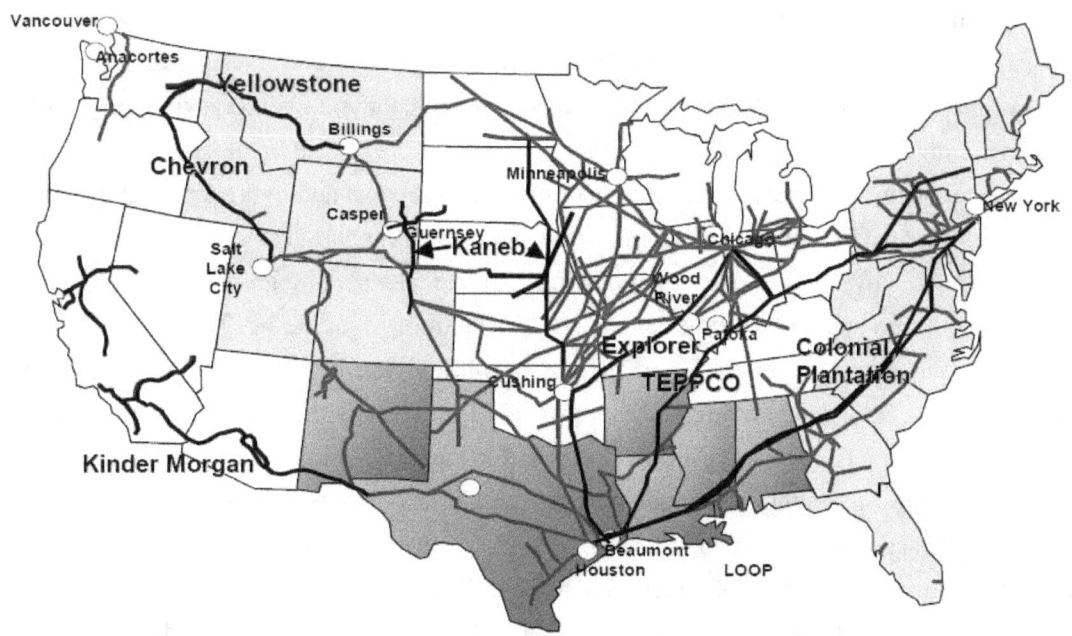

Source: Allegro Energy Group

Aside from the domestic refining industry, US refiners face limited competition from abroad. While the US is very dependent on foreign oil, domestic refinery production accounts for about 90% of US gasoline consumption, though the import share has grown since the mid-1990s. These imports come primarily into the Northeast, which receives 45% of its supply from outside sources, such as the US Virgin Islands, the United Kingdom, the Netherlands, and Canada.

2.1 Capacity and Utilization of US Oil Refineries

The refining industry consists of 142 refineries owned by 61 refining companies in January 2011. However, no new complex refineries have been built in the US since 1976.[18] In fact, many plants have closed and the number of refineries has fallen from 223 in 1985. However, most of these closures were small and inefficient plants, and those that remain have expanded, so total operable capacity has grown from 15.6 million barrels per day (bpd) in 1985 to over 18 million bpd today (atmospheric distillation capacity). The overall number of refineries along with their production capacity are displayed in figure 5. The average plant size has increased from 74,000 bpd in 1985 to almost 128,000 bpd in 2011. The largest refiner (Exxon Mobil) controls about 10% of the total US refining capacity and the top five refiners account for 43% of total capacity.

Though the atmospheric distillation capacity of oil refineries is the most often cited figure when talking about the size of plants, consideration of the capacity of downstream units is also important as refiners seek maximum flexibility in their production slate. Figure 6 displays the average size of downstream refining units as a proportion of total downstream capacity by PADD. While there are other downstream units, such as hydrotreaters and vacuum distillation units, these four units make up a majority the typical refinery's downstream capacity. (Fluid) Catalytic Cracking units make up the largest percentage of downstream capacity for all five PADDs. These units break up heavy gas oils into smaller and more valuable molecules. Catalytic reformers are the next largest group of units and these are generally used to increase the octane level of petroleum products. Instead of breaking down molecules like a cracker, reformers reconfigure molecules to make them more valuable. Thermal cracking and catalytic hydrocracking are the smallest of the downstream units, though used relatively more in PADD V. These also break apart chains of hydrocarbons into smaller chains either using heat (thermal) or using a catalyst and hydrogen (hydrocracking). One extreme form of thermal cracking is known as coking, which breaks apart heavy feedstocks into lighter oils. Hydrocrackers are relatively more efficient at making distillate than making gasoline.[19]

Capacity utilization rates at US refineries had been rising throughout the 1990s, but have fallen throughout the 2000s to an average of about 85% in 2011 as shown in figure 7.[20] From 2000 to 2008, the average utilization rate in all US manufacturing industries was 77%, so even with the recent drop, refiners still operate their plants at high rates.[21] Also shown in figure 7 is the average utilization rate by month (averaged across years). It is clear that although annual averages have fallen, refiners still run their plants at a high rate during the high-demand summer driving months with utilization rates averaging over 90%. Note these rates are an average across plants, some of which may be shut down for a turnaround, while others are running near their maximum rate. Unfortunately, I do not observe the utilization rate of individual plants.

---

[18] Several small refineries have been built, all with less than 100,000 barrels per day of distillation capacity. See http://www.eia.gov/tools/faqs/faq.cfm?id=29&t=6.

[19] Total downstream capacity as a percentage of upstream distillation capacity (a measure of plant complexity) also varies significantly from 60% in PADD I to 84% in PADDs III and V.

[20] See http://www.eia.gov/dnav/pet/pet_pnp_unc_dcu_nus_m.htm.

[21] See http://www.federalreserve.gov/releases/G17/caputl.htm.

Figure 5: Number of Plants and Capacity over Time

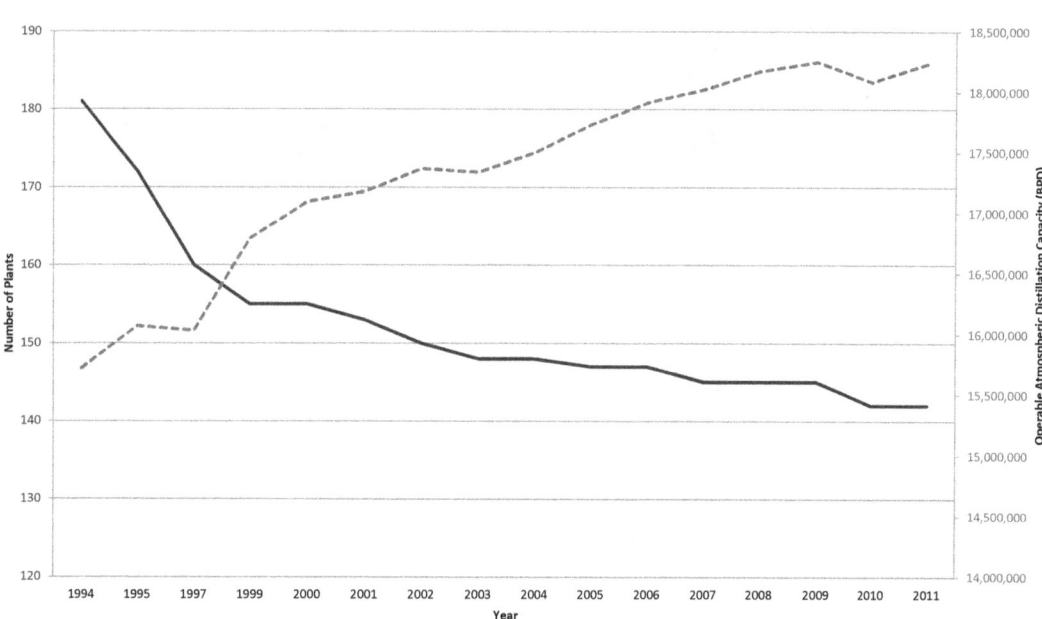

Building a new refinery is very expensive, and environmental requirements and permits create significant hurdles.[22] Evidence from a 2002 US Senate hearing estimated the cost of building a 250,000 bpd refinery at around 2.5 billion dollars, with a completion time of 5-7 years (Senate (2002)). This assumes the various environmental hurdles and community objections are satisfied. In May 2007, the chief economist at Tesoro, Bruce Smith, was quoted as saying that the investment costs in building a new refinery are so high that "you'd need 10 to 15 years of today's margins [at the time, around 50%] to pay it back."[23]

---

[22] One of the few new plants in development is in North Dakota. The 20,000 bpd plant is scheduled to be completed by late 2015.

[23] The National Petrochemical & Refiners Association estimates that the average return on investment in the refining industry between 1993-2002 was 5:5%. The S&P 500 averaged over 12% for the same period. See "Lack of Capacity Fuels Oil Refining Profits" available online at http://www.npr.org/templates/story/story.php?storyId=10554471 (downloaded: 09/13/2008). Crude oil acquisition costs on the West Coast were about $1.30 per gallon in early 2007 compared with wholesales gasoline prices of around $2.00 per gallon (source: EIA).

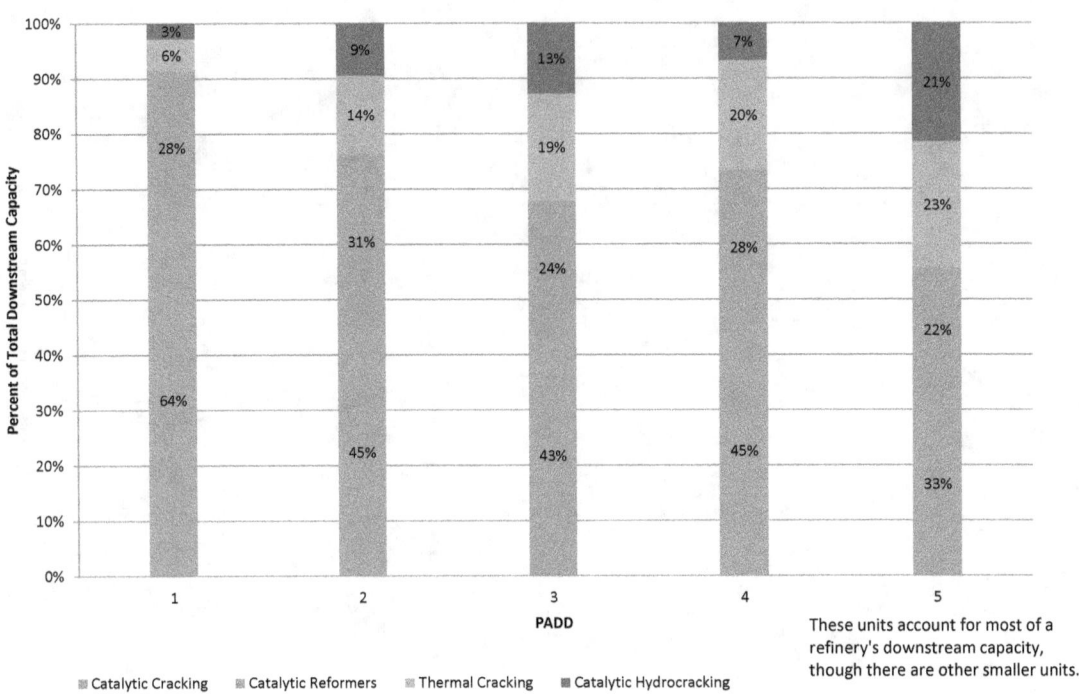

Figure 6: Downstream Capacity by PADD, 2010

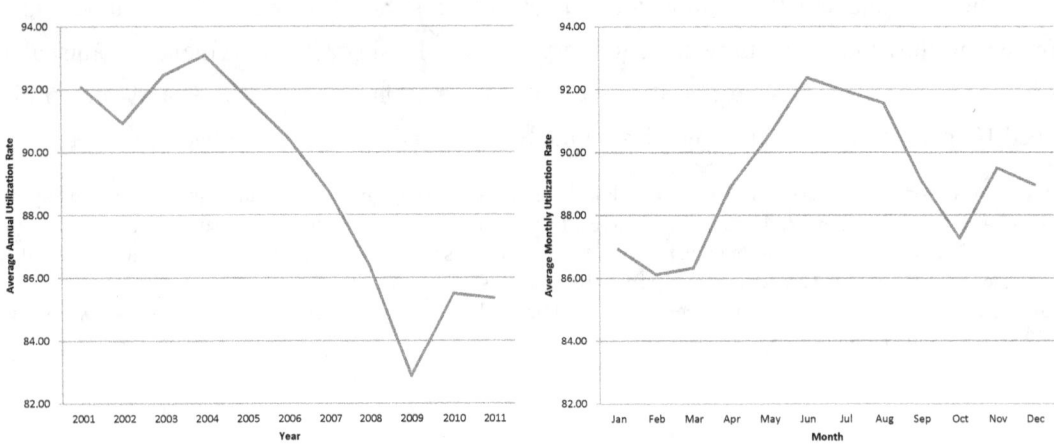

Figure 7: Average Utilization Rates: Annual (L) and Monthly (R)

Even without new refineries, existing refineries have invested to expand capacity.[24] The distribution of historical investments in atmospheric distillation capacity is shown in figure 8. While the mean investment has been 1.3% per year, the median is zero as plants tend to make very infrequent investments. Even restricting the sample to non-zero changes as shown in the graph, investments tend to be small, with almost 85% of the non-zero changes less than 10%. Although almost 75% of plant-year observations in the sample show

---

[24]I observe change in the capacity of different units at a refinery over time, but not the cost to make those changes.

no change in atmospheric distillation capacity, there is some investment in either upstream or downstream units in over 63% of the observations.

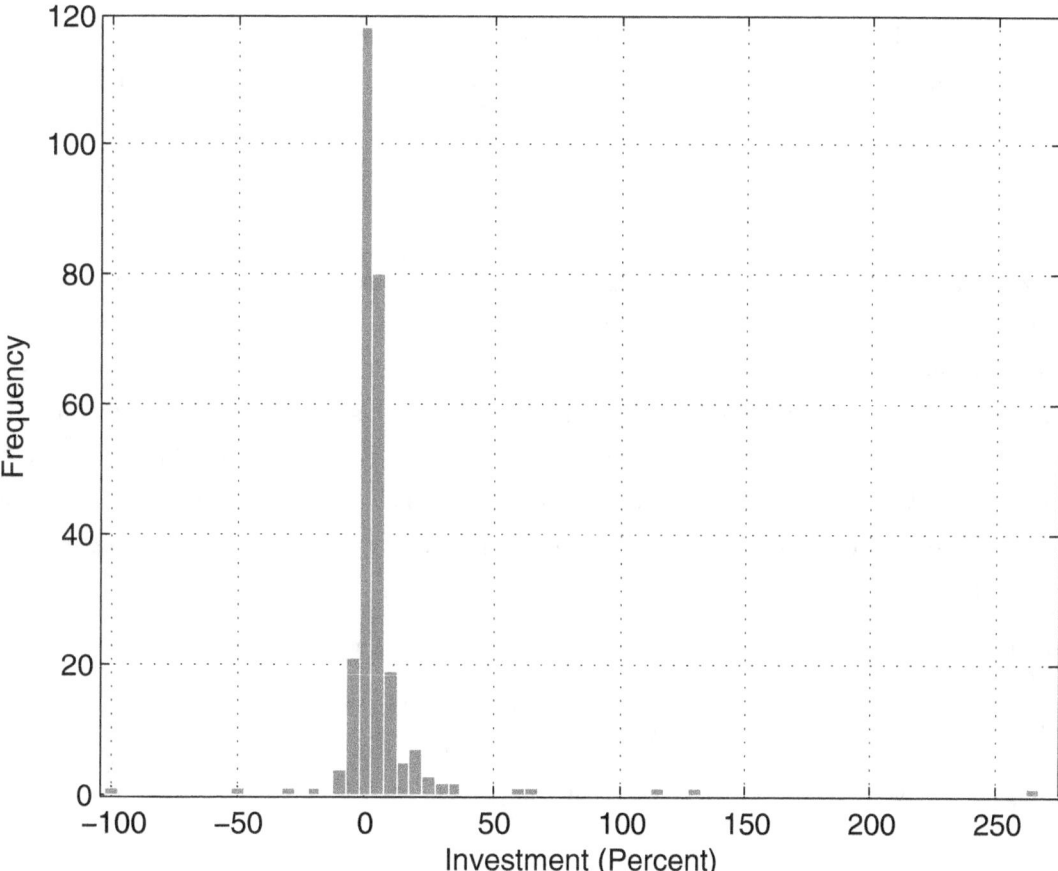

Figure 8: Distribution of Non-Zero Atmospheric Distillation Investments

Aside from the recession of 2008, while total refining capacity has risen in the past 10 years, it has not kept up with demand growth. Capacity of oil refiners has increased by 10% in the past 10 years, while demand for gasoline has increased about 17%. The gap has been filled by new requirements that gasoline be blended with ethanol and to some degree, growing imports. However, new regulations requiring the shift from MTBE[25] oxygenates to ethanol poses a problem for this segment of supply because foreign refiners have not invested in the facilities to produce ethanol-blended gasoline.[26] Even with excess capacity, at certain times of the year supply alternatives can be limited so even a minor supply disruption (or a major one like Hurricane Katrina) can have a large price impact.[27]

---

[25]Methyl Tertiary Butyl Ether.

[26]See http://www.eia.gov/pub/oil_gas/petroleum/feature_articles/2006/mtbe2006/mtbe2006.pdf.

[27]Following Hurricane Katrina on 9/23/05, capacity fell by 5 million bpd. This represented a full one third of US refining capacity. Inventories are also limited as there is only about 20-25 days worth of gasoline in storage at any time.

2.2 Profitability (Crack Spreads)

Although oil refining has historically been an industry plagued by thin profit margins, refiners typically see larger profits when crude oil prices are low and/or product demand is relatively high.[28] Taking into account approximate relative importance of the two leading refined products, gasoline and distillate, that hypothetically might be produced from a single barrel of crude oil, one simple measure of the profit margin at any point in time at a refinery is the "crack spread."[29] The crack spread, expressed in dollars per barrel, is calculated as:

$$Crack = \frac{1*Price(distillate) + 2*Price(gasoline) - 3*Price(crude\ oil)}{3}. \qquad (1)$$

The crack spread for refineries in three states are shown in figure 9. Data are from EIA and are based on the first purchase price of crude oil and wholesales prices of gasoline and distillate in each state.[30] The crack spread fluctuates quite a bit from month to month, generally peaking in the summer months of each year. Refineries in each state may be using very different crude oils. While most refineries use multiple types of crude oil, Brent is relatively more important on the East Coast, WTI in the Midwest, and Alaskan North Slope on the West Coast. Though the crack spreads shown tend to move together, the levels vary and refineries in one area of the country may have better price spreads than in another area and these relationships change over time.

---

[28] See, for example, ftp://www.eia.doe.gov/pub/oil_gas/petroleum/analysis_publications/petroleum_issues_trends_1996/CHAPTER7.PDF.

[29] The most popular crack spread is known as the "3-2-1 crack spread" referring to the approximate ratio of 3 barrels of crude oil to 2 barrels of gasoline and 1 barrel of distillate. Less complex refineries may use other ratios reflecting their typical production levels (e.g., 2-1-1).

[30] See: http://www.eia.gov/dnav/pet/pet_pri_dfp1_k_m.htm and http://www.eia.gov/dnav/pet/pet_pri_refoth_a_epm0_pwg_dpgal_m.htm.

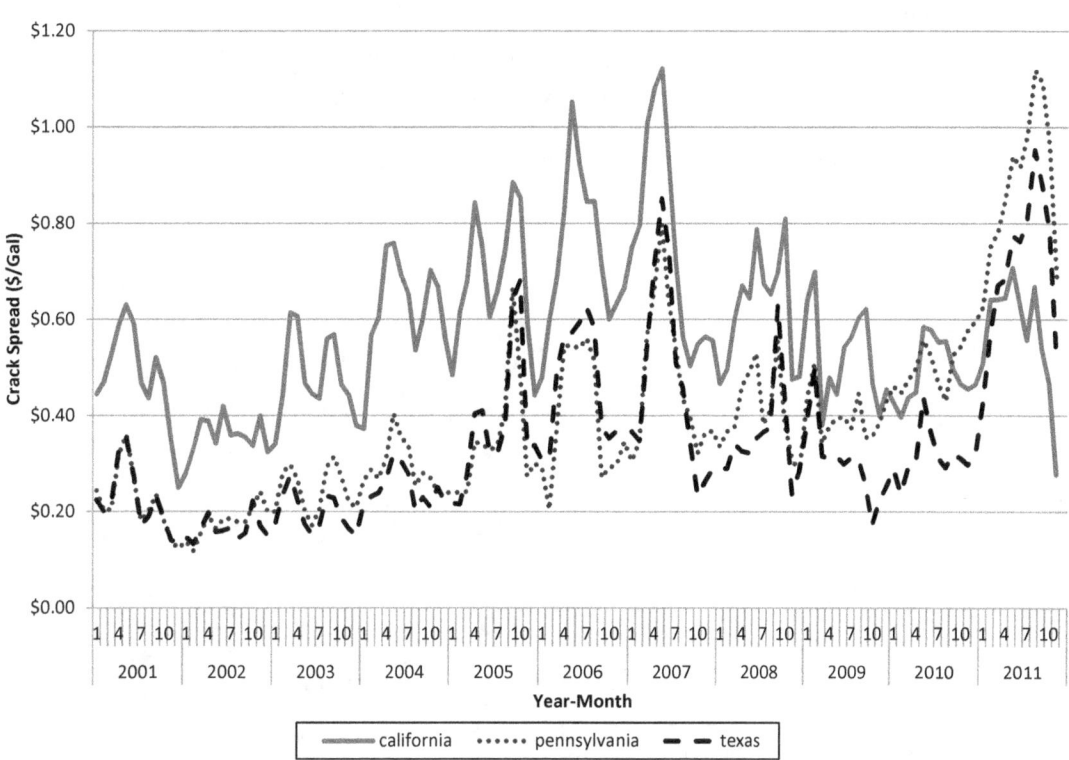

Figure 9: Crack Spreads for Three States

2.3 Refinery Maintenance and Outages

An oil refinery is a complex operation that requires frequent maintenance, ranging from small repairs to major overhauls.[31] The regular maintenance episodes tend to be short and have minimal impact on production as they are strategically scheduled for low demand periods. Unplanned outages, by definition, can take place at any time and can have a major impact on production capability. The EIA divides refinery outages into four classes, summarized in table 1.

Table 1: Refinery Downtime

Type	Typical Length of Outage	Frequency
Planned Shutdowns	1-2 Weeks	Every year
Unplanned Shutdowns	2-4 Weeks	-
Planned turn-arounds	3-9 Weeks	Every 3-5 years
Emergency Shutdowns	Varies	-

Source: EIA.

---

[31] Refinery maintenance is crucial not only for production sustainability, but also for the safety of the plant. A 2005 fire at BP's Texas City refinery killed 15 workers and injured over 100 more.

Planned turn-arounds are major refinery overhauls, while planned shutdowns bridge the gap between turn-arounds. Unplanned shutdowns involve unexpected issues that may allow for some strategic planning of the downtime, but often may force a refinery to reduce production sub-optimally. Finally, emergency shutdowns are those that cause an immediate plant breakdown like a refinery fire.

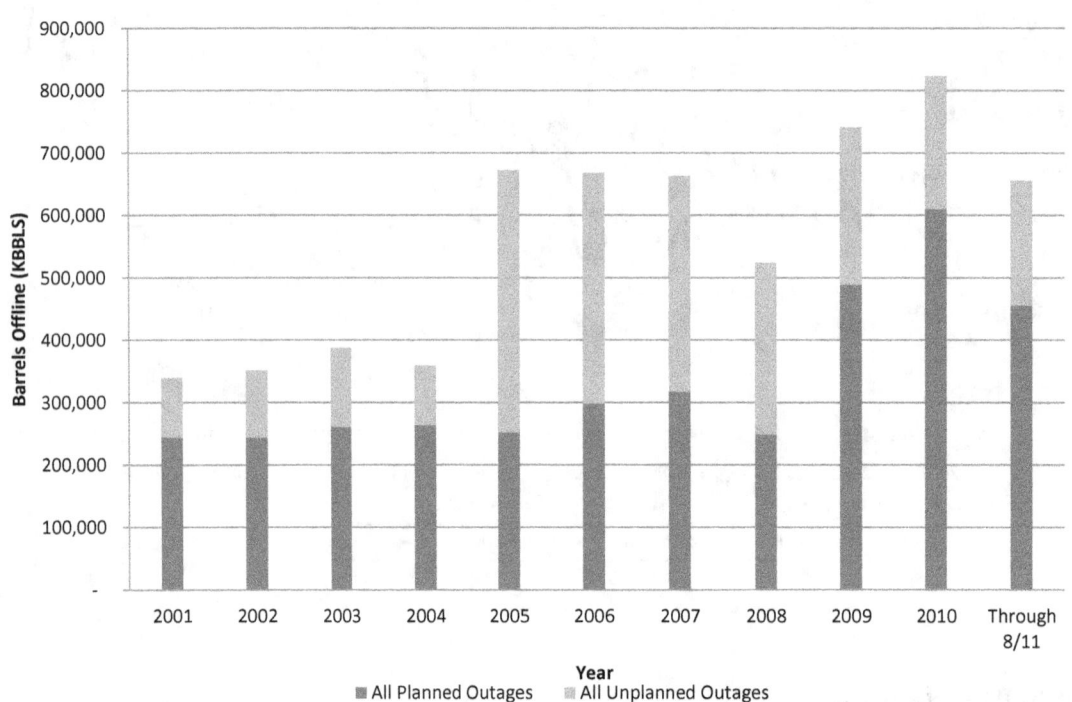

Figure 10: Planned and Unplanned Outages by Year

Organization for planned turn-arounds typically start years in advance, and cost millions of dollars to implement, in addition to the revenue lost from suspending production. Due to the hiring of outside personnel, major refineries often have to plan these turnarounds at different times because of the shortage of skilled labor to implement them. Given the typical seasonal variation in product demand, the ideal periods for maintenance are the first and third quarter of the year, though in some northern refineries, cold winter weather forces shifts in planned downtimes. Figure 10 shows the planned and unplanned outages over time for all US plants. Clearly seen in figure 10 is the increase in unplanned outages following the hurricanes in 2005 and the increase in planned outages in 2009 as refiners went offline for maintenance as demand fell during the recession.

Even though refineries consist of several components, such as distillation columns, reformers and cracking units, these components are dependent on one another so a breakdown of any one component can affect the production capability of the entire refinery. Downstream units include hydrocrackers, reformers, fluid catalytic cracking (FCC) units, alkylation units, and coking units. They are responsible for breaking down hydrocarbons into more valuable products and removing impurities such as sulfur. For example, in a typical refinery, only 5% of gasoline is produced from the primary distillation process; the rest comes hydrocrackers (5%), reformers (30%), FCC and alkylation units (50%), and coking units (10%). Not all refineries have all of these components, so such refineries are even more affected when one component goes down (EIA (2007)).

Figure 11 shows the percent of capacity offline by year and for various refining units. Though the percentages tend to move roughly together, certain units are more affected in some years (e.g., most catalytic hydrocracking capacity is located along the Gulf Coast so was particularly affected by the hurricanes in 2005). Since 2005, typically 5-8% of each unit's capacity is offline in a given year for either planned maintenance or unplanned outages.

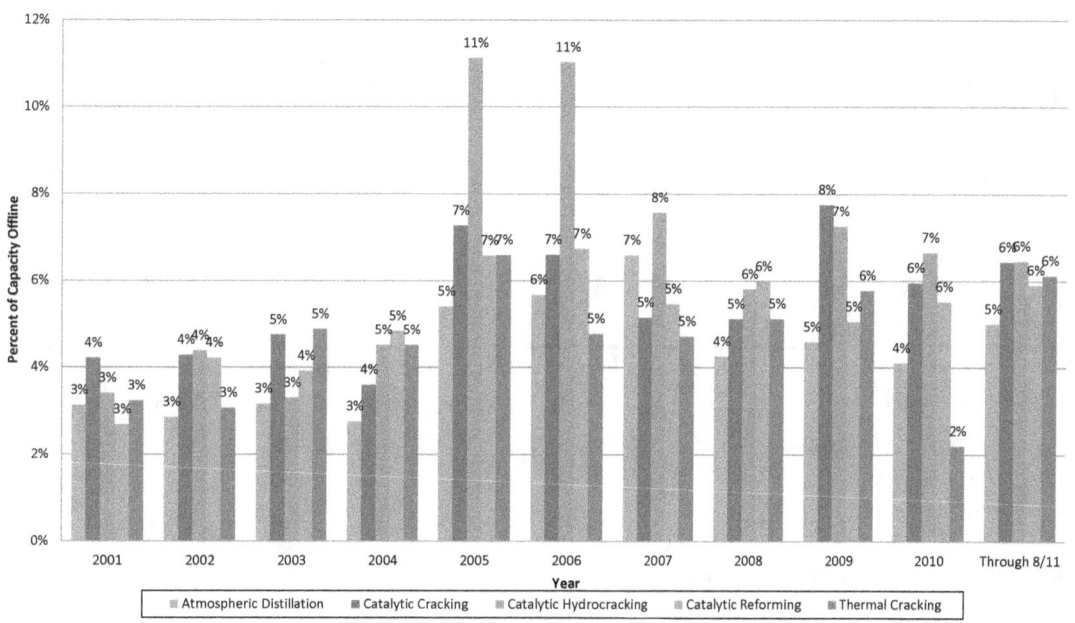

Figure 11: Outages by Unit and Year

At the PADD level, EIA reports that in the 1999-2005 period, refineries experienced reductions in monthly gasoline and distillate production of up to 35% due to outages. At the monthly frequency, there is little effect of outages on product prices. This is primarily because most (planned) outages occur during the low-demand months when markets are not tight; most outages last less than a month; and the availability of imports, increased production from other refineries, and inventories provide a cushion to supply. However, unplanned outages, like those caused by a hurricane, still affect may have significant effects on the downstream prices and profitability of all refineries.

Overall, the oil refining industry features several economic puzzles, some of which I explore in this paper. While the industry is relatively competitive, refiners at times can earn significant profits, as measured by the crack-spread. However, entrants have yet to overcome the regulations and costs of setting up a new plant and existing firms have been cautious in their expansion. As a result, plants may run at high rates of utilization, which leads to instability in the face of unexpected capacity disruptions. These outages can impact both product prices and the investment decisions of refiners.

3 Data

I collect outage data on all refineries from January 2001- August 2011 from Petrocast (Industrial Info Resources). Outage data are available by plant and unit type (atmospheric distillation, FCC, hydrocrackers, reformer, and thermal crackers) and planned and unplanned outages are reported separately. I observe the length of the outage (in days) and the number of barrels that were offline.[32] Descriptive statistics on the outages data are shown in table 2. Of the 13,696 plant-year-month observations in the data, 3,544 contain some type of outage. The average monthly atmospheric distillation outage is around 203,000 barrels.

Table 2: Refinery Outages, 2001-August 2011

	N (>0)	Min	Mean	Max	Std. Dev.
Outages (KBPM)					
All	3,544	0	457	28,943	1,646
Atmospheric Distillation	1,564	0	203	14,203	869
Catalytic Cracking	1,441	0	91	5,425	397
Catalytic Hydro-Cracking	687	0	30	3,720	198
Catalytic Reforming	1,572	0	52	4,340	247
Thermal Cracking	814	0	30	4,340	182

Descriptive statistics reported at the plant-year-month level in thousands of barrels per month for each unit from 2001 - August 2011. There are a total of 13,696 observations (107 plants * 128 months).

I match the outage data with investment data that is publicly available from the US Energy Information Administration (EIA). The data reflect the current atmospheric distillation capacity of the plant, but also the capacities of the downstream units mentioned above. Capacity data is available at an annual level and descriptive statics for 2010 are shown in table 3. Almost all plants in the database have atmospheric distillation and reforming capacity and most have catalytic cracking units.[33] Investments in physical capacity are infrequent given the high costs of taking units offline while the changes are made. Therefore annual data is appropriate for measuring these changes, however smaller increases in capacity throughput (known as "capacity creep") may occur throughout the year. Since EIA and Petrocast do not share a common plant identifier, I manually match plants between the two datasets based on their name and location, which results in a database containing 107 plants and representing about 92% of total US refining capacity.

---

[32]There are other potentially interesting dimensions to the data that I plan to exploit in future work. I mention a few in section 5.
[33]Of the 107 plants in the database, 103 are active in 2010.

Table 3: Plant Capacities, 2010

	N (>0)	Min	Mean	Max	Std. Dev.
Capacity (BPD)					
Atmospheric Distillation	103	6,500	161,296	584,000	122,438
Catalytic Cracking	84	0	55,086	243,000	51,621
Catalytic Hydro-Cracking	43	0	16,570	130,000	25,140
Catalytic Reforming	91	0	33,120	146,000	30,811
Thermal Cracking	56	0	23,311	122,000	29,684

Descriptive statistics reported at the plant level in barrels per day for each unit in 2010.

Finally, I collect refiner wholesale prices of gasoline, distillate (diesel fuel), and first-purchase prices of crude oil from which I create a simple 3-2-1 crack spread described in section 2.[34] Both the crude oil and product prices are usually available at the state-level so all refineries in a given state are matched to the same set of prices. For states that EIA does not report a crude oil price, I use the corresponding PADD price. In some regressions below, I also use PADD-level gasoline and distillate prices that are averages of the state-level prices. Gasoline prices are a sales-weighted average price of all grades sold by refiners. Gasoline and distillate stocks (available at the PADD level) and utilization rates (available at the refining district level) are also matched to the data.[35]

Descriptive statistics on utilization rates, prices, and refinery stocks are shown in table 4. Utilization rates during my sample average about 89% of atmospheric distillation capacity and crude prices average 58 dollars per barrel (though peak around $134 in 2008). The crack spread experiences considerable variability over the sample period, ranging from 20 cents up to almost one dollar per gallon.

---

[34] EIA defines a first-purchase price as "An equity (not custody) transaction involving an arms-length transfer of ownership of crude oil associated with the physical removal of the crude oil from a property (lease) for the first time. A first purchase normally occurs at the time and place of ownership transfer where the crude oil volume sold is measured and recorded on a run ticket or other similar physical evidence of purchase."

[35] PADDs I, II, and III are further divided into several sub-districts. Data are available here:
capacity: http://www.eia.gov/petroleum/refinerycapacity/
product prices: http://www.eia.gov/dnav/pet/pet_pri_refoth_dcu_nus_m.htm
crude prices: http://www.eia.gov/dnav/pet/pet_pri_dfp1_k_m.htm
utilization Rates: http://www.eia.gov/dnav/pet/pet_pnp_unc_dcu_nus_m.htm
stocks:http://www.eia.gov/dnav/pet/pet_stoc_wstk_a_epm0_sae_mbbl_m.htm.

Table 4: Utilization Rates, Prices, and Stocks, 2001-August 2011

	N	Min	Mean	Max	Std. Dev.
Utilization Rate (%)					
Atmospheric Distillation	128	80.19	89.16	97.35	4.21
Prices ($/Gal)					
WTI Crude	128	0.46	1.39	3.19	0.64
Brent Crude	126	0.45	1.37	3.16	0.68
Gulf Conventional Gas	126	0.50	1.57	3.28	0.70
Gulf Distillate (Heaing Oil)	126	0.52	1.61	3.80	0.77
Crack Spread	128	0.20	0.44	0.98	0.16
Stocks (KBPM)					
Gasoline	128	190,020	210,605	235,157	9,595
Distillate	128	97,181	132,881	172,731	18,288

Descriptive statistics reported at the year-month level from 2001 - August 2011. Some prices through June 2011. Converting to other units, the average price of WTI is about 58 dollars per barrel and the crack spread has averaged about 18.6 dollars per barrel over the sample.

4 Empirical Specifications and Results

In the following section, I outline my empirical specifications and results regarding the relationships between oil refinery outages, profitability, utilization and investment. I first consider planned outages and how they are affected by profitability and time-of-year effects. Then I move to unplanned outages and consider how the intensity at which a plant is running and the time since the last maintenance episode affect the likelihood of future outages. Once I understand the causes of outages, I then turn to their effect on prices, specifically considering how the current tightness of the market as measured by utilization rates and product stocks affect the impact of outages on prices. The last empirical specification brings everything together to determine how planned and unplanned outages, utilization rates, and crack spreads affect the investment decisions of refiners.

4.1 Planned Outages

"Do refiners generally take planned downtime for maintenance when profit margins are low and do they delay taking their plants offline when margins are high?" To answer these questions, I estimate the following regression:

$$Pr(PlannedOutage_{jm}) = \beta_0 + \beta_1(CrackSpread_m) + \mu_m + \varepsilon_{jm}. \tag{2}$$

Planned outages by refinery j in month m are regressed on the state-level crack spread and month fixed effects.[36] I estimate a simple probit regression predicting the probability of a planned outage, running separate models for all outages, atmospheric distillation outages, and outages at major downstream refining units. Controlling for month effects is crucial because it is well know that plants take annual maintenance in the low-demand periods (usually early spring and again in the fall) and my goal is to estimate the effect of the crack spread changing throughout the year.

Table 5: Probit Results: Pr(Planned Outage)

Dependent Variable:	Any Planned Outages (1/0)		Planned Atmos. Dist. Outages (1/0)		Planned Cat. Crack Outages (1/0)	
Variable:	Coeff.	t-stat	Coeff.	t-stat	Coeff.	t-stat
Constant	-0.686***	14.451	-1.307***	21.858	-1.391***	20.774
Crack ($/Gal)	-0.456***	7.151	-0.214***	2.662	-0.449***	4.622
Month FE	Yes		Yes		Yes	
Observations	13,807		13,807		13,807	
McFadden R^2	0.04		0.03		0.05	

Dependent Variable:	Planned Cat. HydroCrack		Planned Reformer Outages (1/0)		Planned Thermal Cracking Outages	
Variable:	Coeff.	t-stat	Coeff.	t-stat	Coeff.	t-stat
Constant	-1.990***	22.806	-1.232***	20.930	-1.910***	22.406
Crack ($/Gal)	0.084	0.790	-0.336***	4.195	-0.147	1.509
Month FE	Yes		Yes		Yes	
Observations	13,807		13,807		13,807	
McFadden R^2	0.02		0.04		0.02	

An observation is a plant-month for 107 plants from January 2001 - August 2011. 3-2-1 crack spread based on state-level first-purchase prices of crude oil, gasoline, and distillate for each plant. The dependent variable is an indicator variable that equals one if a planned outage occured on the specified unit in a given month.

Results of this regression are shown in table 5. The coefficient on the crack spread is negative and significant when considering the probability of any planned outage meaning that relatively more profitable periods are associated with fewer planned outages. The coefficient on the crack spread continues to be negative and statistically significant in the specifications for atmospheric distillation, catalytic cracking, and reformer outages, while it is insignificant for catalytic hydrocracking and thermal cracking units. The crack spread is a rough measure of refinery profitability measuring only the relationship between the price of crude oil and two refined products (gasoline and heating oil) so other prices and constraints may be important for downstream units that primarily produce other products.

---

[36]The crack spread is one measure of the opportunity cost of shutting down the refinery. Since the outage itself may lead to higher product prices and a larger crack spread, the contemporaneous crack spread may overstate this cost. However, including the crack spread in the previous month produces similar results.

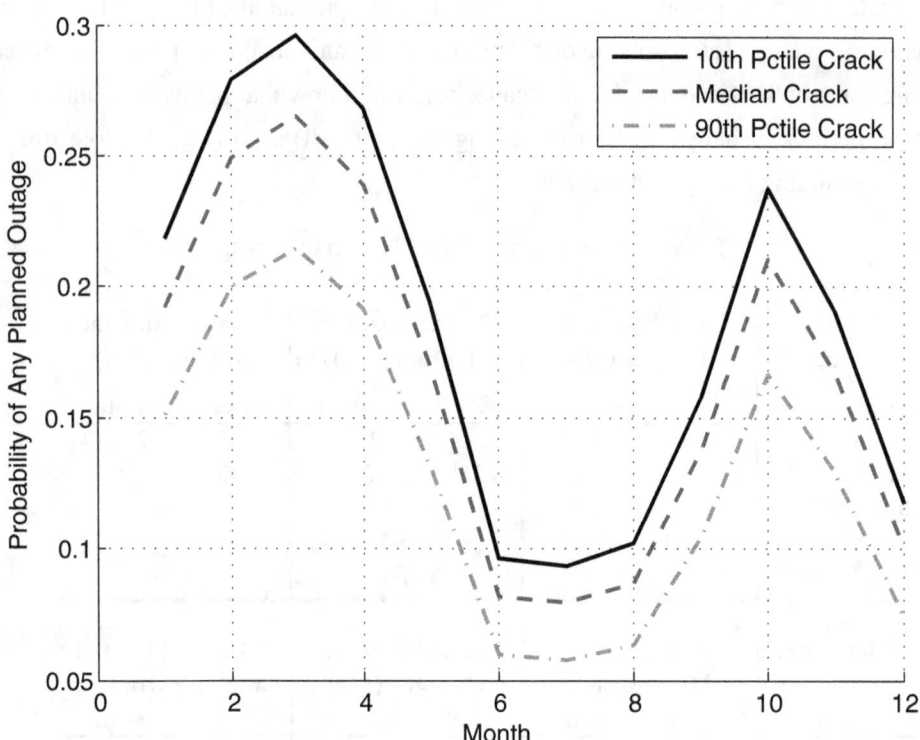

Figure 12: Probit Marginal Effects: Planned Outages by Month

Interpreting the magnitude of these coefficients is easier by considering the marginal effects. In figure 12, I plot the marginal effects by the month of the year. The graph shows the strong seasonality in predicted planned outages, peaking in May and again in October. I evaluate these effects at three different levels of the crack spread: the 10th, 50th and 90th percentiles. The higher crack spreads are associated with a lower predicted probability of a planned outage. Figure 13 shows the marginal effects of varying the crack spread for three different months of the year. The predicted probability of a planned outage ranges from over 0.3 when crack spread is low to less than 0.05 when the crack spread is relatively high.

Figure 13: Probit Marginal Effects: Planned Outages by Crack Spread

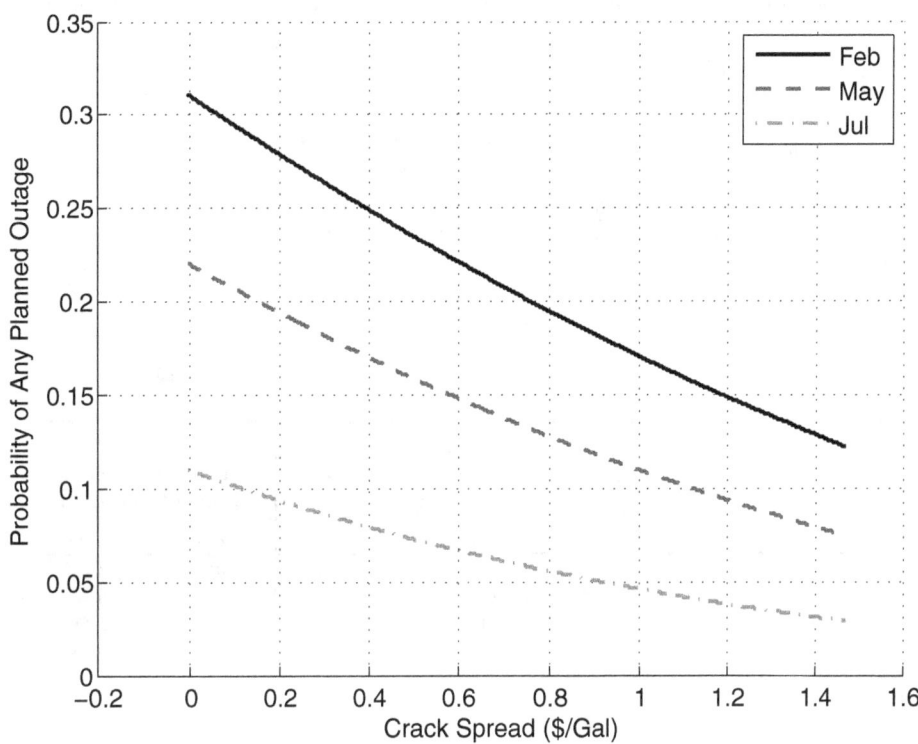

4.2 Unplanned Outages

Next, I move on to the question, "How are unplanned outages affected by utilization rates and the time since the last plant turn-around?" Unfortunately, utilization rates are only measured at the refinery district level so are an imperfect proxy for the production intensity of any given plant. They also measure only the atmospheric distillation utilization, which is an important unit at a refinery, but only one of many that is involved in the production process. In light of this limitation, I estimate the following regression:

$$Pr(UnplannedOutage_{jm}) = \beta_0 + \beta_1(Utilization_{m-1}) + \beta_2(TSLTA_{jm}) \qquad (3)$$
$$+ \beta_3(Hurricane_{pm}) + \mu_m + \varepsilon_{jm}.$$

Again, a probit model is estimated predicting the probability of an unplanned outage at refinery j in month m. The variable TSLTA measures the time since the last turnaround in months. I calculate this time using the last planned outage of the atmospheric distillation unit at a given plant. Turn-arounds generally involve complete plant shut downs so planned atmospheric distillation outages are a good indicator of turn-arounds.[37] Hurricanes and other major weather events may cause many plants to experience an unplanned outage at the same time. Therefore, I include and indicator that equals one if the PADD in which the plant

---
[37] For robustness, I have also used both the time since the last planned FCC and hydrocracker outage and the results are similar.

is located is impacted by a hurricane during the month of the reported outage.[38] Month fixed effects are included to control for seasonality of unplanned outages not accounted for by the hurricane indicator.

Table 6: Probit Results: Pr(Unplanned Outage)

Dependent Variable:	Any Unplanned Outages (1/0)		Unplanned Atmos. Dist. Outages (1/0)		Unplanned Cat. Crack Outages (1/0)	
Variable:	Coeff.	t-stat	Coeff.	t-stat	Coeff.	t-stat
Constant	-0.074	0.383	0.198	0.818	-0.760***	3.312
Utilization Rate (%)	-0.014***	6.607	-0.023***	8.646	-0.010***	4.215
Time Since Last T/A	0.003***	3.063	0.003***	2.951	0.003***	3.295
Hurricane ID	0.791***	10.526	0.992***	11.884	0.911***	11.105
Month FE	Yes		Yes		Yes	
Observations	13,721		13,721		13,721	
McFadden R^2	0.02		0.05		0.03	

Dependent Variable:	Unplanned Cat. HydroCrack Outages (1/0)		Unplanned Reformer Outages (1/0)		Unplanned Thermal Cracking Outages (1/0)	
Variable:	Coeff.	t-stat	Coeff.	t-stat	Coeff.	t-stat
Constant	-0.160	0.546	0.037	0.151	-0.659**	2.166
Utilization Rate (%)	-0.023***	7.444	-0.021***	7.766	-0.017***	5.089
Time Since Last T/A	0.005***	3.909	0.002	1.466	0.005***	3.532
Hurricane ID	0.911***	9.489	0.964***	11.513	0.910***	9.745
Month FE	Yes		Yes		Yes	
Observations	13,721		13,721		13,721	
McFadden R^2	0.05		0.05		0.05	

An observation is a plant-month for 107 plants from January 2001 - August 2011. "Time Since Last T/A" measures the number of months since the plant last experienced a planned outage (or Turn-Around). Utilization rate measured at the refining district level. "Hurricane ID" equals one if a hurricane made landfall in the PADD in which the plant is located in a particular month. The dependent variable is an indicator variable that equals one if a unplanned outage occured on the specified unit in a given month.

Results of this regression are presented in table 6. The TSLTA and hurricane variables are consistently positive and significant as expected. However, the utilization rate is estimated to be negative and significant in all specifications. This is likely because the rate is measured at the PADD-district level and a large outage may affect all plants in a district over multiple months. While the hurricane variable will control for contemporaneous weather-related effects, a widespread outage in a prior month may result in lower district-level utilization rates in the current month as plants take time to come back online.

---

[38] Data on past hurricanes is collected from the National Oceanic and Atmospheric Administration:http://www.aoml.noaa.gov/hrd/hurdat/All_U.S._Hurricanes.html.

Figure 14: Probit Marginal Effects: Unplanned Outages by Time Since Last T/A

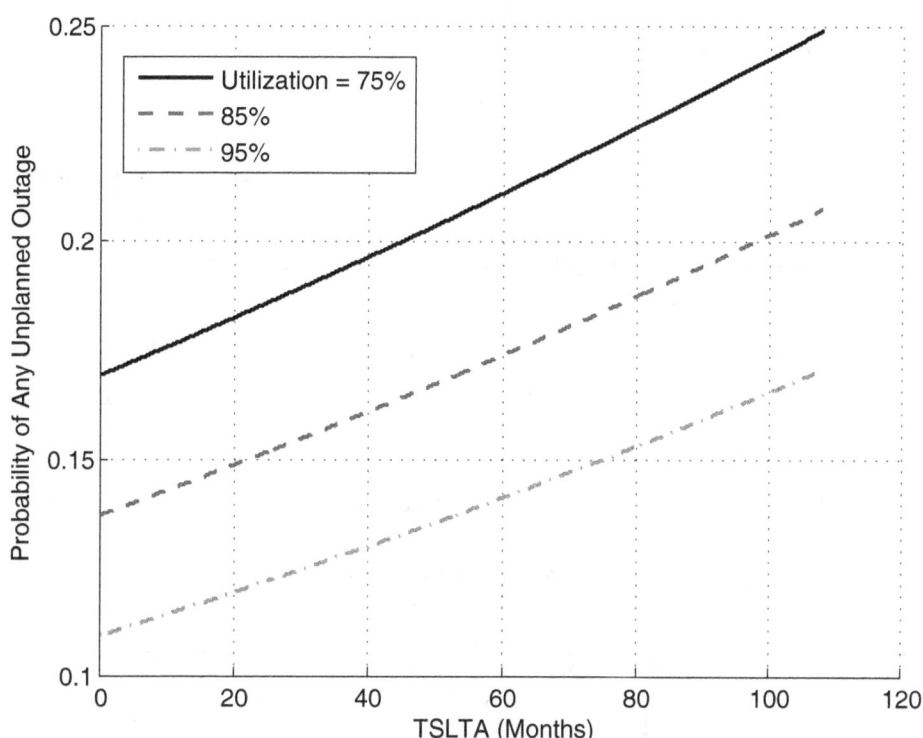

Again, the magnitude of the effects are better seen with a graph of the marginal effects. Figure 14 shows the predicted probability of an unplanned outage as a function of the time since the last planned plant turn-around.[39] This effect is increasing though lower for higher utilization rates, ranging from about 0.10 for plants that have recently performed maintenance to 0.25 for plants that have not experienced a planned turn-around in 8-9 years.[40] Unfortunately, most of the data are not rich enough to separate unplanned outages due to weather from those due to mechanical problems.

4.3 Product Prices

The last two subsections showed that planned outages tend to occur during the spring and fall and during times of relatively low margins as measured by the crack spread. The amount of time since the last plant turn-around is positively associated with future unplanned outages. But the question then becomes, "Do these outages have an effect on prices?" An outage that occurs during a time when inventories are relatively high and/or nearby utilization rates are low, should have less of an effect on output prices than when the

---

[39]Figure 18 in the appendix shows the marginal effects as they vary by the district-level utilization rate.

[40]The data are not rich enough to show planned turn-arounds that are spurred on by unplanned outages, but for robustness I calculate the TSLTA variable based on the time since the last outage (of any type) and the results are similar. Note, the mean and median time since the last planned atmospheric distillation outage are 17.5 and 13 months respectively. 8-9 years is the longest spell in the data without a planned turn-around. The 75th percentile of TSLTA is just over two years.

market is relatively tight. Therefore, I estimate the following regression equation using OLS:

$$GasolinePrice_{pm} = \beta_0 + \beta_1(CrudePrice_{pm}) + \beta_2(Hurricane_{p,m-1}) + \beta_3(Outages_{pm}) \quad (4)$$
$$+ \beta_4(GasolineStocks_{pm}) + \mu_m + \mu_y + \mu_p + \varepsilon_{pm}.$$

Since wholesale prices are generally determined by supply and demand forces beyond those in individual states (due to pipelines, imports, etc.), I run this regression on gasoline prices at the PADD-month level. The independent variables include the crude oil price, aggregate outages in the PADD, an indicator for a hurricane impacting the PADD in the previous month, and gasoline stocks. Month and PADD fixed effects are also included to account for seasonality and any geographic variation in the level of prices unrelated to outages respectively. Year fixed effects are included to account for exogenous changes in gasoline price levels over time. I also run the model on distillate prices.

Table 7: OLS Results: Effects of Outages on Prices - Planned versus Unplanned

Dependent Variable:	Gasoline Price ($/Gal)		Gasoline Price ($/Gal)		Distillate Price ($/Gal)		Distillate Price ($/Gal)	
Variable:	Coeff.	t-stat	Coeff.	t-stat	Coeff.	t-stat	Coeff.	t-stat
Constant	0.510***	5.141	0.495***	4.913	0.180***	3.579	0.190***	3.757
Crude Price ($/Gal)	0.927***	50.204	0.928***	50.207	0.992***	56.999	0.993***	56.627
Hurricane ID (m-1)	0.025	0.780	0.029	0.912	0.015	0.496	0.016	0.513
Planned Atmos Capacity Offline (%)	0.003*	1.765			0.004***	2.921		
Unplanned Atmos Capacity Offline (%)	0.005***	2.604			0.002	1.080		
Planned FCC Capacity Offline (%)			0.003	0.986			0.002	0.597
Unplanned FCC Capacity Offline (%)			0.010**	2.529			0.004	1.211
Gas Stocks (Mbbls)	-0.005***	3.253	-0.005***	3.081				
Distillate Stocks (Mbbls)					-0.002***	2.580	-0.002**	2.548
Month FE	Yes		Yes		Yes		Yes	
Year FE	Yes		Yes		Yes		Yes	
PADD FE	Yes		Yes		Yes		Yes	
Observations	635		635		635		635	
R^2	0.98		0.98		0.98		0.98	

An observation is a padd-year-month covering January 2001 - August 2011. Gasoline, distillate, and crude oil prices are state-level first-purchase prices matched to each plant. Plant outages are aggregated to the padd-month level.

Table 7 presents results of four specifications run on gasoline and distillate prices using either atmospheric distillation outages or FCC (fluid catalytic cracking) outages. In each regression, I include planned and unplanned outages separately to determine if product prices are less sensitive to planned outages. The results clearly show that the variation in the crude oil price is the primary driver of the level of gasoline and distillate prices with coefficients very close to one. The gasoline price regressions also show that unplanned atmospheric distillation outages have a positive and significant effect on prices, and the effect is almost twice as large as the effect of planned outages. The results are similar for FCC outages with the coefficient on unplanned outages over three times the size the coefficient on planned outages (the latter coefficients are not statistically significant). Gasoline stocks have an expected negative and significant association with prices and the hurricane indicator is not significant, though crude oil prices and the month fixed effects likely pick up much of the variation in prices caused by weather-related shocks.

Table 8: OLS Results: Effects of Outages on Prices - By Refining Unit

Dependent Variable:	Gasoline Price ($/Gal)		Distillate Price ($/Gal)	
Variable:	Coeff.	t-stat	Coeff.	t-stat
Constant	0.519***	5.188	0.195***	3.891
Crude ($/Gal)	0.925***	50.018	0.990***	57.060
Hurricane ID (m-1)	0.022	0.690	0.008	0.259
Atmos Cap Offline (%)	0.005***	2.837	0.005***	3.361
CatCrack Cap Offline (%)	0.004	1.416	0.000	0.111
CatHydroCrack Cap Offline (%)	0.003	0.375	-0.009	1.166
Reformer Cap Offline (%)	-0.017**	2.525	-0.017***	2.695
Thermal Cracking Cap Offline (%)	0.005	0.783	0.016**	2.534
Gas Stocks (Mbbls)	-0.006***	3.397		
Distillate Stocks (Mbbls)			-0.002***	2.834
Month FE	Yes		Yes	
Year FE	Yes		Yes	
PADD FE	Yes		Yes	
Observations	635		635	
R^2	0.980		0.98	

An observation is a padd-year-month covering January 2001 - August 2011. Gasoline, distillate, and crude oil prices are state-level first-purchase prices matched to each plant. Plant outages are aggregated to the padd-month level.

The distillate price regressions show that planned atmospheric distillation outages are positively associated with distillate prices and FCC outages show no significant effect. The FCC unit is relatively more important for gasoline production so this result is not unexpected though it is surprising that unplanned atmospheric outages show no significant effect. To better account for the fact that a refinery is composed of many refining units and each is more or less important for producing gasoline and distillate, I run two regressions of prices on the outages of individual refining units. These results are presented in table 8. The results show that atmospheric distillation and catalytic cracking have the largest positive effect on gasoline prices and thermal cracking is also important for distillate prices. In both specifications, the coefficient on reformer outages is negative and significant. Recall the gasoline price is a sales-weighted average of all grades (octane levels) of gasoline sold by refiners and reformers are used to increase the octane level of gasoline. Therefore, if the reformer goes down, plants may end up producing more (lower octane) regular grade gasoline, depressing the weighted-average price.

Figure 15: The Effects of Outages on Gas Prices: By Utilization Rate

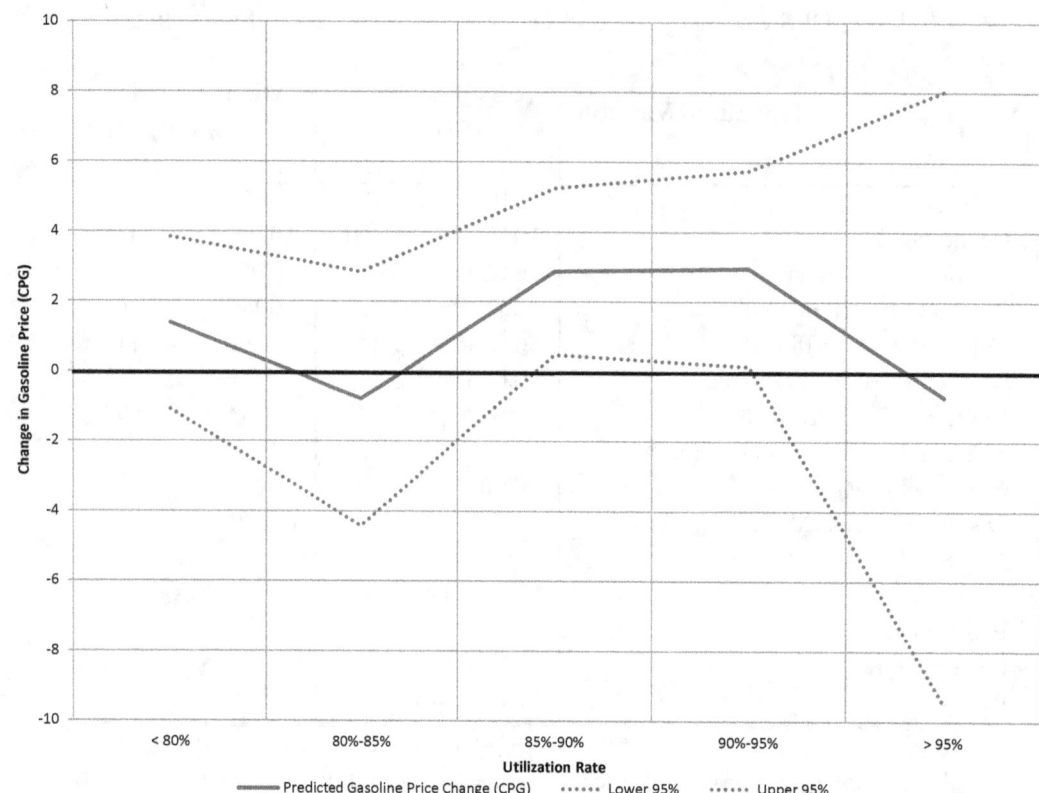

Predicted change in the gasoline price from an average outage of atmospheric distillation capacity at different utilization rates.

In figure 15, I show the estimated price effect of atmospheric distillation outages and how the effect varies with the prevailing utilization rate.[41] Confidence intervals on the estimated coefficient are also shown on the graph. The estimates are generally increasing in the utilization rate indicating that outages that occur during periods of high utilization rates have more of an effect on prices than when utilization rates are low. The economic importance of these results can be seen by estimating the predicted effect on prices for typical outages seen in the real world. For example, at a utilization rate between 90% and 95%, if an average atmospheric distillation outage occurred (about 4.15% of a PADD's capacity), the model predicts that gasoline prices would rise by 1.5 cents per gallon. When utilization rates are between 80% and 85% (the 2012 average was 87.5%), the same outage would have no statistically significant effect on gasoline prices.[42]

---

[41] I estimate equation 4 interacting outages with indicators for months when the utilization rate in the PADD-district was less than 80%, between 80% and 85%, between 85% and 90%, etc. Of course outages cause the utilization rate to fall so I select the months in each regression based on the utilization rate just prior to an outage.

[42] The first estimate is found by multiplying the predicted effect (0.35 cpg) by the size of an average outage measured as the percent of a PADD's capacity (4.15).

Table 9: Gasoline Price Effects of an Average Outage

Specification	Outage Type	Average PADD Capacity (BPD)	Average Outage (BPD)	Average Outage (%)	Coeff. Estimate	Predicted Price Effect (CPG)	95% C.I.
A	Atmospheric Distillation Unit	3,395,525	141,058	4.15%	0.352	1.46	(0.48, 2.45)
B	Planned		83,064	2.45%	0.268	1.11	(-0.13, 2.35)
	Unplanned		58,006	1.71%	0.480	1.99	(0.49, 3.49)
C	Catalytic Cracking Unit	1,151,442	62,782	5.45%	0.580	3.16	(0.53, 5.80)
D	Planned		34,515	3.00%	0.311	1.70	(-1.68, 5.08)
	Unplanned		28,267	2.45%	1.003	5.47	(1.22, 9.72)
	By Unit (Planned+Unplanned)						
	Atmospheric Distillation	3,395,525	141,058	4.15%	0.465	1.93	(0.59, 3.27)
E	Catalytic Cracking	1,151,442	62,782	5.45%	0.410	2.24	(-0.87, 5.34)
	Catalytic Hydro Cracking	344,020	20,851	6.06%	0.313	1.89	(-8.02, 11.80)
	Reformer	684,763	35,992	5.26%	-1.698	-8.92	(-15.86, -1.98)
	Thermal Cracking	486,775	21,120	4.34%	0.534	2.32	(-3.50, 8.13)

Regressions are run on data at the PADD-month level from January 2001 - December 2011. Prices are regressed on the crude oil price, the percent of the PADD's capacity that is offline, a hurricane indicator, gasoline stocks, and month, year, and PADD fixed effects. Separate regressions are run on each specification above (indicated in column 1). The predicted price effect in specification A is found as follows: the model predicts that a 1% atmospheric distillation outage in a PADD-month is associated with a 0.352 CPG increase in the gasoline price. An average outage in a PADD-month is 4.154% of the total PADD capacity, so an average outage is predicted to raise gasoline prices by 0.352*4.15 = 1.46 CPG.

In table 9, I calculate the predicted price effects of an average outage of each refining unit.[43] I also consider planned and unplanned outages separately for the main distillation unit and the catalytic cracking unit. As expected, planned outages of the distillation and catalytic cracking units are not associated with a significant price effect because they tend to occur during periods of relatively low gasoline demand in the spring and fall (see figure 12). In contrast, unplanned outages of these two units have a positive and significant effect on prices with an average unplanned outage to a refinery's catalytic cracking unit associated with a 5.47 cpg gasoline price increase. In specification (E), planned and unplanned outages of five important refining units are all included in the same regression. While coefficients on all units except the reformer are positive, only the coefficient on atmospheric outages is positive and significant. The coefficient on reformer outages is negative and significant as in table 8, possibly due to more lower octane gasoline being produced as a result of the outage.

One way to interpret these predicted price effects is to compare them to what one would expect given estimates of the price elasticity of demand for gasoline. Following an average PADD outage of 4.15%, my predicted price effect in specification (A) is 1.46 cpg, or 0.93% of the average gasoline price observed during the sample period. If there were no other supply responses, these price and quantity changes would imply a price elasticity of demand estimate of -4.46. This estimate is far more elastic than estimates in the literature, which are generally around -0.2, and suggests that overall output does not fall by nearly as much due to offsetting output reactions by operating plants and inventory management. In fact, the reduction in output that is consistent with an elasticity of -0.2 and a 0.93% price increase is 0.186%, which implies that over 95% of the average PADD outage was offset.

---

[43] Specifications (B) and (D) of Table 9 correspond to the first two specifications of Table 7 and specification (E) corresponds to the first specification in Table 8. For brevity, Table 9 shows only the coefficients corresponding to different types of outages. All regressions control for the crude oil price, hurricanes, inventories and include month, year and PADD fixed effects. Specifications (A) and (C) aggregate planned and unplanned outages.

4.4 Investment

The last set of regressions consider how planned and unplanned outages, utilization rates, profitability and recent investments by competing plants affect the future investment behavior of refiners. Investment is measured as the change in capacity (in barrels) at a plant from one year to the next. I expect that refinery investment should be positively related to the prior year utilization rate and crack spread while negatively related to recent increases in refined products stocks and investment by competing plants.[44] Outages may lead to more investment in the future if they make it more likely for a plant to perform investments because the plant is already shut down.

I estimate the investment relationship in two stages. I first investigate the extensive margin: a refiner's decision whether to make any positive investment in capacity. I create an indicator variable that equals one if a plant's capacity rises from one year to the next and estimate the following probit model:[45]

$$
\begin{aligned}
Pr(Investment_{jy} > 0) = \ & \Phi\big(\beta_0 + \beta_1(CrackSpread_{s,y-1}) \\
& + \beta_2(Utilization_{d,y-1}) + \beta_3(Utilization_{d,y-1} * Hurricane_{p,y-1}) \\
& + \beta_4(PlannedAtmosOutages_{j,y-1}) + \beta_5(PlannedAtmosOutages_{j,y-2}) \\
& + \beta_6(UnplannedOutages_{j,y-1}) + \beta_7(UnplannedOutages_{j,y-1} * Hurricane_{p,y-1}) \\
& + \beta_8(\Delta GasolineStocks_{p,y-1}) + \beta_9(CompetitorInvestment_{p,y-1}) \\
& + \mu_y + \varepsilon_{jy}\big).
\end{aligned}
\tag{5}
$$

Investment in capacity by plant j in year y is regressed on last year's average crack spread (at the state level), the PADD subdistrict utilization rate, planned and unplanned outages, inventories, and investment by other plants in the same PADD. I interact the utilization rate and unplanned outages with a hurricane indicator that equals one if the PADD in which the plant is located experienced a hurricane in the prior year. I also include the change in planned outages in the prior two years because investments may take multiple years to complete and prior planned outages may contribute to the investment process. Year fixed effects are included to control for the interest rate that may be changing over time and affecting a refiner's investment decision.[46]

In stage two, I investigate the intensive margin: a refiner's decision over how large of an investment in capacity to make, conditional on making any positive investment. This stage is operationalized by running a regression of the change in capacity on the same set of explanatory variables as above, restricting the sample to only those plant-year observations where investment is positive. I estimate the following equation by OLS:

---

[44] I calculate competitor investment as the change in capacity by other plants located in the same PADD. A binary indicator that equals one when competitor investment is positive is used in the empirical specifications.

[45] I focus only on positive investments in capacity because less than 5% of observations show a reduction in capacity.

[46] While it may be tempting to use refined product and crude oil futures prices as an independent variable in this regression, several papers have shown that futures prices provide no additional predictive power over current prices. See, for example, Wu and McCallum (2005) and Alquist and Kilian (2008).

$$
\begin{aligned}
(Investment_{jy}|Investment_{jy} > 0) ={} & \beta_0 + \beta_1(CrackSpread_{s,y-1}) \\
& + \beta_2(Utilization_{d,y-1}) + \beta_3(Utilization_{d,y-1} * Hurricane_{p,y-1}) \\
& + \beta_4(PlannedAtmosOutages_{j,y-1}) + \beta_5(PlannedAtmosOutages_{j,y-2}) \\
& + \beta_6(UnplannedOutages_{j,y-1}) + \beta_7(UnplannedOutages_{j,y-1} * Hurricane_{p,y-1}) \\
& + \beta_8(\Delta GasolineStocks_{p,y-1}) + \beta_9(CompetitorInvestment_{p,y-1}) \\
& + \mu_y + \varepsilon_{jy}.
\end{aligned} \quad (6)
$$

Results of the extensive margin regression are shown in table 10. The five specifications presented correspond to the atmospheric distillation unit and the four downstream refining units. Coefficients on planned outages in the previous two years are positive and significant as expected in most specifications, while unplanned outages show no significant effect except for the thermal cracking specification. Recent investment by competing plants is negative and significant for the atmospheric distillation unit suggesting that plants may be reacting to the increase in PADD capacity by holding off on expanding their own plant.[47] The utilization rate is positive and strongly significant in the first two specifications, which implies that all else equal, plants are more likely to expand capacity if plants in their refining district are running at a high rate. It is surprising that the coefficients on the crack spread are negative and significant for three of the units. One potential explanation is mean reversion: refiners expect profitability to fall to more typical levels in years following large crack spreads.

---

[47] Further robustness checks show this effect is strongest in PADD I. Aside from PADD V, refiners in PADD I ship the smallest quantity of refined products to other PADDs so plants may be less likely to expand if nearby plants also recently made investments.

Table 10: Probit Results: Investment, Extensive Margin

Variable:	Dependent Variable:	I(Invest > 0), Atmospheric Dist. Unit Coeff.	t-stat	I(Invest > 0), Catalytic Cracking Coeff.	t-stat
Constant		-3.937**	2.522	-5.455***	3.133
Crack Spread ($/Gal,y-1)		-0.849*	1.925	-1.025**	2.051
Utilization Rate (%,y-1)		0.040**	2.322	0.054***	2.855
Utilization Rate(%,y-1)*Hurricane		0.000	0.213	0.000	0.123
Planned Unit Outages (%,y-1)		0.007	1.056	0.033***	3.322
Planned Unit Outages (%,y-2)		-0.005	0.628	0.022**	2.023
Unplanned Unit Outages (%,y-1)		-0.010	0.643	-0.013	0.671
Unplanned Unit Outages(%,y-1)*Hurricane		0.013	0.607	0.032	1.369
Gasoline Stocks(%Chg,y-1)		-0.001	0.067	-0.007	0.364
Competitor Investment(Indicator,y-1)		-0.316*	1.808	-0.220	1.434
Year FE		Yes		Yes	
Observations		904		900	
R^2		0.05		0.07	

Variable:	Dependent Variable:	I(Invest > 0), Cat. Hydro Cracking Coeff.	t-stat	I(Invest > 0), Cat. Reformer Coeff.	t-stat	I(Invest > 0), Thermal Cracking Coeff.	t-stat
Constant		-3.196	1.477	-3.820**	2.138	-1.485	0.791
Crack Spread ($/Gal,y-1)		0.811	1.459	-0.562	1.115	-1.744***	2.906
Utilization Rate (%,y-1)		0.014	0.578	0.030	1.541	0.008	0.376
Utilization Rate(%,y-1)*Hurricane		0.004*	1.709	0.000	0.003	0.002	0.936
Planned Unit Outages (%,y-1)		0.034**	2.114	0.019*	1.702	0.068***	5.497
Planned Unit Outages (%,y-2)		0.068***	4.295	0.008	0.629	0.070***	5.369
Unplanned Unit Outages (%,y-1)		-0.001	0.083	-0.030	0.771	0.029**	2.185
Unplanned Unit Outages(%,y-1)*Hurricane		0.030	1.564	0.028	0.681	-0.034	1.137
Gasoline Stocks(%Chg,y-1)		0.020	0.786	-0.031	1.551	0.030	1.324
Competitor Investment(Indicator,y-1)		-0.028	0.184	0.264*	1.828	-0.110	0.694
Year FE		Yes		Yes		Yes	
Observations		909		886		892	
R^2		0.05		0.03		0.11	

The dependent variable equals one if a plant increased its capacity in year y. An observation is a plant-year for 107 plants from 2002 - 2011. Some plants are not observed in all years. 3-2-1 crack spread is the prior year average based on state-level first-purchase prices of crude oil, gasoline, and distillate for each plant. Utilization rate is the prior year average for the refining district in which the plant is located. Gasoline stocks measure the PADD-level change in stocks from y-2 to y-1. Competitor Investment is an indicator that equals one if capacity by other refiners in the plant's PADD increased in the previous year. Hurricane is an indicator that equals one if the plant is located in a PADD that experienced a hurricane the previous year.

Results of the intensive margin regression are shown in table 11. The estimated coefficients on the crack spread and competitor investment for the atmospheric distillation unit remain negative and significant, while planned outages are positively associated with investment for four of the five units. However, other types of outages on the various refining units do not show a consistent or significant effect. Because investment is measured as the change in capacity at each unit, it is possible that refiners are investing in improvements to their refining units that do not effect capacity, such as, increasing their ability to process different types of crude oil or improving their flexibility in adjusting their production slate.

Table 11: OLS Results: Investment, Intensive Margin

Dependent Variable:	(Invest|Invest > 0), Atmospheric Dist. Unit		(Invest|Invest > 0), Catalytic Cracking	
Variable:	Coeff.	t-stat	Coeff.	t-stat
Constant	-2.724	0.172	2.311	0.531
Crack Spread ($/Gal,y-1)	-10.983**	2.203	-0.100	0.068
Utilization Rate (%,y-1)	0.109	0.639	-0.010	0.202
Utilization Rate(%,y-1)*Hurricane	-0.004	0.235	-0.001	0.344
Planned Unit Outages (%,y-1)	0.127*	1.800	0.045*	1.855
Planned Unit Outages (%,y-2)	0.025	0.356	0.102***	3.742
Unplanned Unit Outages (%,y-1)	-0.049	0.186	-0.071	0.960
Unplanned Unit Outages(%,y-1)*Hurricane	0.253	0.802	0.165**	2.105
Gasoline Stocks(%Chg,y-1)	0.121	0.582	0.059	1.178
Competitor Investment(Indicator,y-1)	-4.005**	2.417	-0.302	0.902
Year FE	Yes		Yes	
Observations	194		153	
R^2	0.16		0.26	

Dependent Variable:	(Invest|Invest > 0), Cat. Hydro Cracking		(Invest|Invest > 0), Cat. Reformer		(Invest|Invest > 0), Thermal Cracking	
Variable:	Coeff.	t-stat	Coeff.	t-stat	Coeff.	t-stat
Constant	-10.048	0.662	2.763	0.323	-6.544	0.847
Crack Spread ($/Gal,y-1)	0.094	0.024	-1.906	0.701	2.028	0.824
Utilization Rate (%,y-1)	0.091	0.551	-0.009	0.103	0.071	0.866
Utilization Rate(%,y-1)*Hurricane	-0.003	0.242	-0.003	0.353	0.010	1.445
Planned Unit Outages (%,y-1)	-0.064	0.683	0.089*	1.654	0.079*	1.845
Planned Unit Outages (%,y-2)	-0.091	1.141	-0.014	0.211	0.053	1.214
Unplanned Unit Outages (%,y-1)	-0.003	0.020	-0.031	0.096	-0.018	0.455
Unplanned Unit Outages(%,y-1)*Hurricane	0.057	0.337	0.030	0.092	0.149	1.251
Gasoline Stocks(%Chg,y-1)	0.493***	2.756	0.179**	1.971	0.011	0.119
Competitor Investment(Indicator,y-1)	1.521	1.218	-0.764	1.100	-0.043	0.074
Year FE	Yes		Yes		Yes	
Observations	77		123		117	
R^2	0.38		0.18		0.14	

The dependent variable is the change in capacity (in barrels) from year y-1 to year y. An observation is a plant-year for 107 plants from 2002 - 2011. Some plants are not observed in all years. 3-2-1 crack spread is the prior year average based on state-level first-purchase prices of crude oil, gasoline, and distillate for each plant. Utilization rate is the prior year average for the refining district in which the plant is located. Gasoline stocks measure the PADD-level change in stocks from y-2 to y-1. Competitor Investment is an indicator that equals one if capacity by other refiners in the plant's PADD increased in the previous year. Hurricane is an indicator that equals one if the plant is located in a PADD that experienced a hurricane the previous year.

5 Conclusion

The focus of this paper was measuring the effect of refinery outages on product prices and investment. It is well known that crude oil prices are the primary driver of gasoline and other petroleum product prices. However, I have shown that outages at refineries, both planned and unplanned, are associated with changes in prices and the future investment decisions of refiners. Refineries are extremely complicated operations and understanding how their operations and outages affect the price we pay for gasoline is difficult to determine. However, with detailed data on both the capacities and outages of individual refining units, I find that depending on the current market conditions (prevailing utilization rates and crack spread), refinery outages can have an economically significant effect on product prices.

As expected, planned outages tend to occur during the low-demand periods and when crack spreads are less favorable for production, while unplanned outages are more likely to occur after prolonged spells between planned plant maintenance. Product prices are positively associated with outages, though the effect varies with the type of outage and the level of tightness in the market as measured by the utilization rate and product stocks. Finally, I showed that investment in certain refining units is positively associated with recent outages to those units, but the effect is insignificant for other units suggesting that there are other considerations affecting a refiner's decision to invest in capacity. These likely include long-term forecasts of product demand, crude oil supply and prices, and a regulatory environment that is constantly changing and affecting a plant's profitability.

There are several directions for future work exploiting a few of the unique features of the dataset. The outage data includes information about planned outages that have been rescheduled or postponed. This may allow me to better estimate how refiners respond to economic conditions as they determine when to perform their planned maintenance. For more recent data (2009-2011), I also observe the reason for the outage (planned turn-around, economic conditions, etc), which could help further identify outages that are likely to have a more significant impact on product prices. Finally, understanding how outages affect refinery investment, both in production capacity and the complexity of refining units, is an important area for future research, particularly given the importance of gasoline and other refined petroleum products to the U.S. economy.

References

1. Aguirregabiria, V. P. Mira, (2006). "Sequential estimation of dynamic discrete games." *Econometrica*, 75(1).

2. Alquist, Ron and Lutz Kilian (2008). "What Do We Learn from the Price of Crude Oil Futures?" *Journal of Applied Econometrics*, 25 (2010): 539-573.

3. Attanasio, Orazio, (2000). "Consumer Durables and Inertial Behavior: Estimation and Aggregation of Ss Rules for Automobiles." *Review of Economic Studies*, October.

4. Bacon, Robert W., (1991). "Rockets and Feathers: The Asymmetric Speed of Adjustment of UK Retail Gasoline Prices to Cost Changes." *Energy Economics*, July.

5. Bajari, Patrick, Lanier Benkard, and Jonathan Levin, (2007). "Estimating Dynamic Models of Imperfect Competition." *Econometrica*, 75(5).

6. Benkard, Lanier, (2004). "A dynamic analysis of the market for wide-bodied commercial aircraft." *Review of Economic Studies*, 71(3).

7. Besanko, David and Ulrich Doraszelski, (2004). "Capacity Dynamics and Endogenous Asymmetries in Firm Size." *The RAND Journal of Economics*, Vol. 35, No. 1. Spring.

8. Besanko, David A., Ulrich Doraszelski, Lauren Xiaoyuan Lu, and Mark A. Satterthwaite, (2008). "Lumpy Capacity Investment and Disinvestment Dynamics." Harvard Institute of Economic Research Discussion Paper No. 2154 Available at SSRN: http://ssrn.com/abstract=1117991.

9. Borenstein, S., C. A. Cameron and R. Gilbert, (1997). "Do Gasoline Prices Respond Asymmetrically to Crude Oil Price Changes?" *Quarterly Journal of Economics*, 112(1).

10. Borenstein, S., (1991). "Selling Costs and Switching Costs: Explaining Retail Gasoline Margins." *The RAND Journal of Economics*, 22(3).

11. Borenstein, S., Andrea Shepard (1996). "Dynamic Pricing in Retail Gasoline Markets." *The RAND Journal of Economics*, 27(3).

12. Chesnes, Matthew (under review). "Asymmetric Pass-Through in US Gasoline Prices."

13. Energy Information Administration, US Department of Energy, (2011). "Market Assessment of Planned Refinery Outages."

14. Energy Information Administration, US Department of Energy, (2008). "A Primer on Gasoline Prices." Online: http://www.eia.doe.gov/bookshelf/brochures/gasolinepricesprimer/index.html [Downloaded: 09/11/2008].

15. Ericson, Richard, and Ariel Pakes, (1995). "Markov-Perfect Industry Dynamics: A Framework for Empirical Work." *Review of Economic Studies*, 62:1, 53-83.

16. Espey, Molly, (1996). "Explaining Variation in Elasticity of Gasoline Demand in the United States: A Meta Analysis." *The Energy Journal*, 17.

17. The Federal Trade Commission, (2006). "Investigation of Gasoline Price Manipulation and Post-Katrina Gasoline Price Increases." Spring.

18. Goldberg, Pinelopi K. and Rebecca Hellerstein, (2008). "A Structural Approach to Explaining Incomplete Exchange-Rate Pass-Through and Pricing-to-Market." *The American Economic Review*, 98(2).

19. The Government Accountability Office, (2006). "Energy Markets: Factors Contributing to Higher Gasoline Prices." GAO-06-412T. February.

20. Gron, Anne, Deborah Swenson, (2000). "Cost Pass-Through in the US Automobile Market." *The Review of Economics and Statistics*, 82(2).

21. Hamilton, James D., (1983). "Oil and the Macroeconomy since World War II." *The Journal of Political Economy*, 91(2).

22. Hastings, Justine, Jennifer Brown, Erin Mansur, and Sofia Villas-Boas, (2008). "Reformulating Competition? Gasoline Content Regulation and Wholesale Gasoline Prices." *Journal of Environmental Economics and Management*, January.

23. Hotz, V. J., and R. A. Miller, (1993). "Conditional Choice Probabilities and the Estimation of Dynamic Models." *Review of Economic Studies*, 60(3).

24. Hubbard, Glenn, (1986). "Supply Shocks and Price Adjustment in the World Oil Market." *The Quarterly Journal of Economics*, 101(1).

25. ICF Consulting, (2005). "The Emerging Oil Refinery Capacity Crunch: A Global Clean Products Outlook."

26. Knittel, Christopher, Jonathan E. Hughes, and Daniel Sperling, (2008). "Evidence of a Shift in the Short-Run Price Elasticity of Gasoline Demand." *The Energy Journal*, 29(1), January.

27. Kreps, David M., Jose A. Scheinkman, (1983). "Quantity Precommitment and Bertrand Competition Yield Cournot Outcomes." *The Bell Journal of Economics*, 14(2), Autumn.

28. Lewis, Matt, (forthcoming). "Asymmetric Price Adjustment and Consumer Search: an Examination of Retail Gasoline Market," forthcoming in *Journal of Economics and Management Strategy*.

29. Lidderdale, T.C.M. (United States Energy Information Administration), (1999). "Environmental Regulations and Changes in Petroleum Refining Operations." Online: http://www.eia.doe.gov/emeu/steo/pub/special/enviro.html [Downloaded: 12/07/2007].

30. Noel, Michael D., (2007). "Edgeworth Price Cycles, Cost-Based Pricing, and Sticky Pricing in Retail Gasoline Markets." *Review of Economics and Statistics*, Vol. 89.

31. Pakes, Ariel, (2000). "A framework for applied dynamic analysis in I.O." Working paper no. 8024, NBER, Cambridge.

32. Pakes, Ariel, Michael Ostrovsky, and Steven T. Berry, (2004). "Simple estimators for the parameters of discrete dynamic games (with entry/exit examples)." Harvard Institute. Economic Research Discussion Paper No. 2036, May.

33. Pakes, Ariel and P. McGuire, (1994). "Computing Markov-perfect Nash equilibria: Numerical implications of a dynamic differentiated product model." *The RAND Journal of Economics*, 25(4).

34. Peterson, D. J. and Sergej Mahnovski, (2003). "New Forces at Work in Refining: Industry Views of Critical Business and Operations Trends." Santa Monica, CA : *The RAND Journal of Economics*.

35. Rust, John and Harry Paarsch, (forthcoming). "Valuing Programs with Deterministic and Stochastic Cycles." Forthcoming in the *Journal of Economic Dynamics and Control*.

36. Rust, John, (2008). "Dynamic Programming." The New Palgrave Dictionary of Economics. Second Edition. Eds. Steven N. Durlauf and Lawrence E. Blume. Palgrave Macmillan.

37. Rust, John, (1987). "Optimal Replacement of GMC Bus Engines: An Empirical Model of Harold Zurcher." *Econometrica*, 55:5, 999-1033.

38. Ryan, Stephen, (forthcoming). "The Costs of Environmental Regulation in a Concentrated Industry." Forthcoming in *Econometrica*.

39. Tirole, Jean, (1988). The Theory of Industrial Organization. Cambridge, MA: M.I.T. Press.

40. The United States Senate, (2002). "Gas Prices: How are they Really Set?" Online: http://www.hsgac.senate.gov/download/report_gas-prices-how-are-they-really-set [Downloaded 10/01/2007].

41. Wu, Tao and Andrew McCallum (2005). "Do Oil Futures Prices Help Predict Future Oil Prices?" FRBSF Economic Letter, Number 2005-38.

A The Refining Process

Since the various components of crude oil have different boiling points, a refinery's essential task is to boil the crude oil and separate it into the more valuable components. Figure 16 displays a simplified diagram of a typical refinery's operations.

Figure 16: Refinery Operations

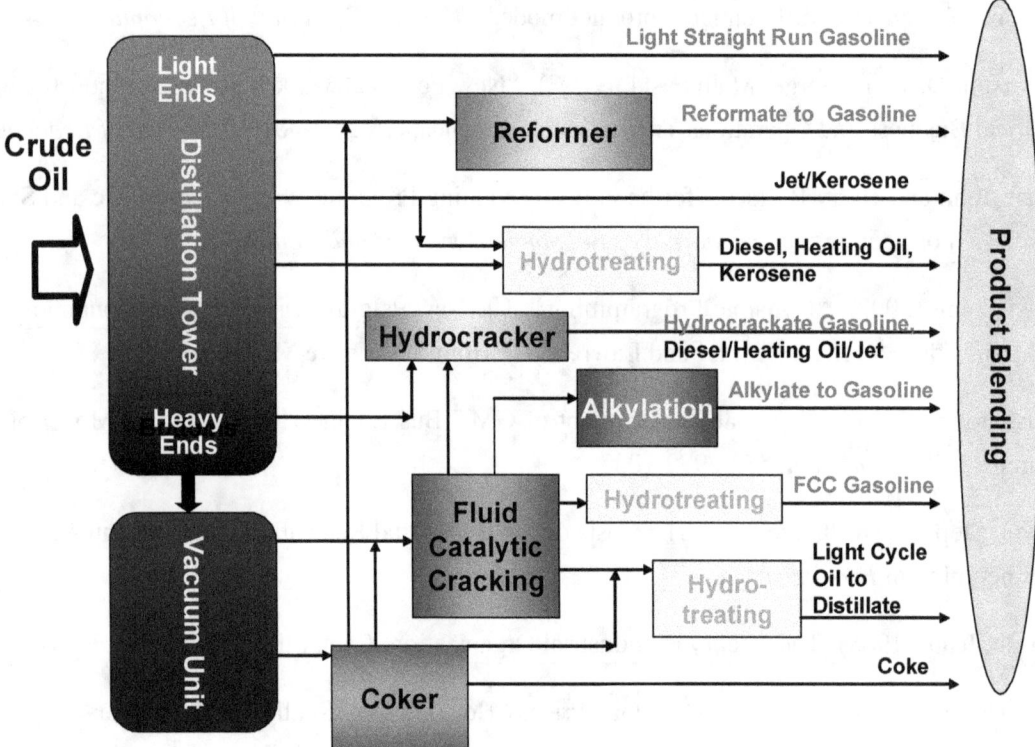

Source: EIA

The first and most important step in the refining process is called fractional distillation. The steps of fractional distillation are as follows:

1. Heat the crude oil with high pressure steam to $1,112°$ fahrenheit.

2. As the mixture boils, vapor forms which rises through the fractional distillation column passing through trays which have holes that allow the vapor to pass through.

3. As the vapor rises, it cools and eventually reaches its boiling point at which time it condenses on one of the trays.

4. The substances with the lowest boiling point (such as gasoline) will condense near the top of the distillation column.

While some gasoline is produced from pure distillation, refineries normally employ several downstream processes to increase the yield of high valued products by removing impurities such as sulfur. Cracking is the process of breaking down large hydrocarbons into smaller molecules through heating and/or adding a catalyst. Cracking was first used in 1913 and thus changed the problem of the refiner from choosing how much crude oil to distill into choosing an appropriate mix of products (within some range). Refineries practice two main types of cracking:

- Catalytic cracking: a medium conversion process which increases the gasoline yield to 45% (and the total yield to 104%).

- Coking/residual construction - a high conversion process which increases the gasoline yield to 55% (and the total yield 108%).

The challenge of choosing the right input and output mix given the available technology creates a massive linear programming problem.

B Crude Oil Quality

Crude oil is a flammable black liquid comprised primarily of hydrocarbons and other organic compounds. The three largest oil producing countries are Saudi Arabia, Russia and the United States.[48] Crude oil is the most important input into refineries and this raw material can vary in its ability to produce refined products like gasoline. The two main characteristics of crude that determine its quality are American Petroleum Institute (API) gravity and sulfur content. The former is a measure (on an arbitrary scale) of the density of a petroleum liquid relative to water.[49] Table 12 summarizes these characteristics and includes some common crude types and their gasoline yield from the initial distillation process.

Worldwide, light/sweet crude is the most expensive and accounts for 35% of consumption. Medium/sour is less expensive and accounts for 50% of consumption while heavy/sour is the least costly and accounts for 15%. Figure 17 show how the average crude oil used by US refiners is becoming heavier and more sour over time though leveling off toward the latter part of the 2000s. This means that the production costs of a gallon of gasoline are changing as refineries must invest in more sophisticated technology in order to process lower quality crude oil.

Since crude oil by itself has very little value to any industry, the price of a barrel of oil reflects the net value of the downstream products that can be created from it. The two major sources of movements in the crude oil price are upstream supply shocks (e.g., due to OPEC's production quotas, international tensions, and hurricanes affecting oil rigs in the Gulf of Mexico) and downstream demand shocks (mainly due to consumer's demand for refined products). The other source often sited by industry experts are refinery inventories of crude oil. Maintaining stocks of crude oil allow the refinery to respond quickly to downstream shocks like an unexpectedly cold winter increasing the demand for heating oil.

---

[48] Production in this sense refers to the quantity extracted from a country's endowment.
[49] Technically, API gravity = (141.5 / specific gravity of crude at $60°$ F) -131.5. Water has an API gravity of $10°$.

Table 12: Crude Qualities

API Gravity	Sulfur Content	
	< 0.7%	> 0.7%
< 22°	Heavy Sweet	Heavy Sour - 14% yield (Maya, Western Canadian)
22° − 38°	Medium Sweet	Medium Sour - 21% yield (Mars, Arab light)
> 38°	Light Sweet - 30% yield (WTI, Brent)	Light Sour

Source: EIA.

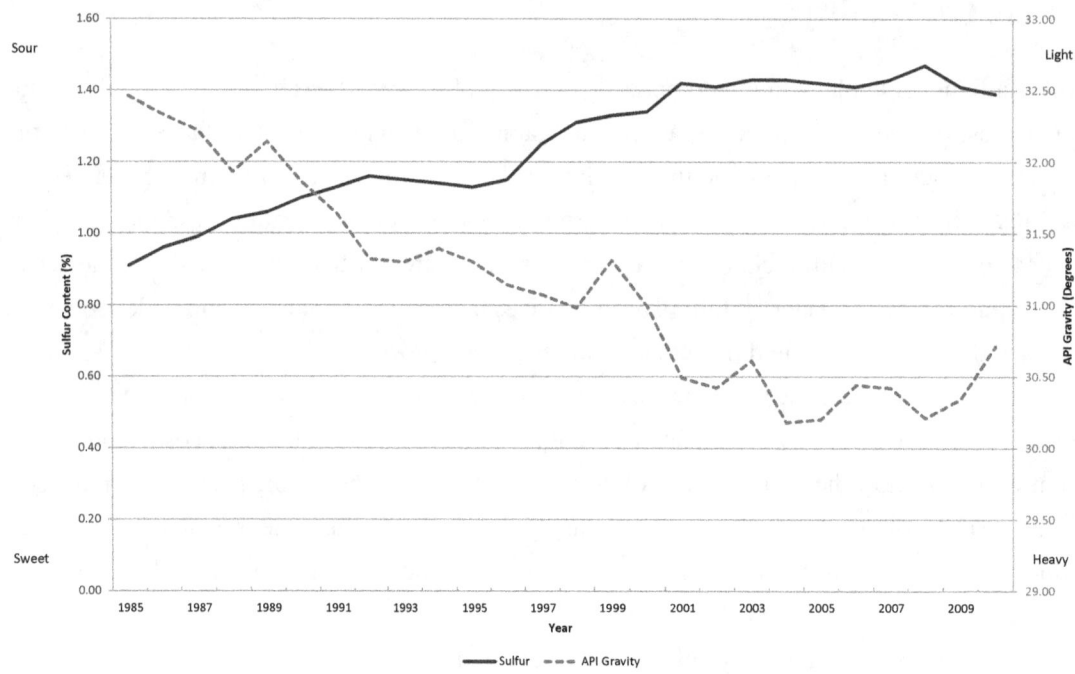

Figure 17: Average Crude Oil Quality: Heavier and Sour

Within the various types of crude oil, the prices of each quality respond differently to shocks. The "light/heavy" differential is one measure that indicates the benefit a refiner can achieve by investing in sophisticated equipment to process heavier crude oil into highly-valued refined products. The differential has varied significantly over the last 10 years from 3 dollars per barrel to almost 20 dollars per barrel. An oil refinery faces a unique decision when making its production choice, one that provides for both flexibility and complexity. One one hand, consumers do not care about the type of crude oil, oxygenates, or distillation process used to make, for example, the gasoline they put in their cars. They just want their car to run well. While this would appear to make a refiner's problem easier, choosing their heterogeneous inputs, such as crude oil, satisfying federal, state and city environmental regulations, and all while maximizing profits, makes for an enormously complex optimization.

C Other Tables and Figures

Table 13: OLS Results: Planned Outages

Dependent Variable:	All Planned Outages/Capacity (%)		All Planned Outages/Capacity (%)		All Planned Outages/Capacity (%)	
Variable:	Coeff.	t-stat	Coeff.	t-stat	Coeff.	t-stat
Constant	0.04	15.99	0.06	12.41	0.02	1.81
Crack ($/Gal)	-0.03	-4.83	-0.02	-3.24	0.01	1.07
Month FE	No		Yes		Yes	
Plant FE	No		No		Yes	
Observations	13,807		13,807		13,807	
R^2	0.001		0.01		0.09	

An observation is a plant-month for 107 plants from January 2001 - August 2011. Refining units included are: atmospheric distillation, catalytic cracking, catalytic hydrocracking, catalytic reformers, and thermal cracking. 3-2-1 crack spread based on state-level first-purchase prices of crude oil, gasoline, and distillate for each plant.

Table 14: OLS Results: Planned Outages by Unit

Dependent Variable:	Planned Atmos. Dist. Outages/Capacity (%)		Planned Cat. Crack Outages/Capacity (%)		Planned Cat. HydroCrack Outages/Capacity (%)	
Variable:	Coeff.	t-stat	Coeff.	t-stat	Coeff.	t-stat
Constant	0.02	1.42	0.00	0.23	0.05	2.82
Crack ($/Gal)	0.02	2.53	0.01	1.72	0.01	0.55
Month FE	Yes		Yes		Yes	
Plant FE	Yes		Yes		Yes	
Observations	13,492		10,967		5,217	
R^2	0.08		0.02		0.04	

An observation is a plant-month for 107 plants from January 2001 - August 2011. 3-2-1 crack spread based on state-level first-purchase prices of crude oil, gasoline, and distillate for each plant. The dependent variable is the percentage of an individual unit's capacity (e.g., catalytic cracking unit) that experiences planned outage in a given month.

Table 15: OLS Results: Unplanned Outages

Dependent Variable:	All Unplanned Outages/Capacity (%)		All Unplanned Outages/Capacity (%)		All Unplanned Outages/Capacity (%)	
Variable:	Coeff.	t-stat	Coeff.	t-stat	Coeff.	t-stat
Constant	0.14	13.45	0.16	14.04	0.16	11.15
Utilization Rate (%)	-0.001	-12.34	-0.002	-13.49	-0.002	-13.86
Time Since Last T/A	0.000	3.32	0.000	3.04	0.000	3.01
Month FE	No		Yes		Yes	
Plant FE	No		No		Yes	
Observations	11,461		11,461		11,461	
R^2	0.02		0.02		0.11	

An observation is a plant-month for 107 plants from January 2001 - August 2011. Refining units included are: atmospheric distillation, catalytic cracking, catalytic hydrocracking, catalytic reformers, and thermal cracking. "Time Since Last T/A" measures the number of months since the plant last experienced a planned outage (or Turn-Around). Utilization rate measured at the refining district level.

Table 16: OLS Results: Unplanned Outages by Unit

Dependent Variable:	Unplanned Atmos. Dist. Outages/Capacity (%)		Unplanned Cat. Crack Outages/Capacity (%)		Unplanned Cat. HydroCrack Outages/Capacity (%)	
Variable:	Coeff.	t-stat	Coeff.	t-stat	Coeff.	t-stat
Constant	0.142	10.018	0.137	7.146	0.291	10.074
Utilization Rate (%)	-0.002	-12.441	-0.002	-8.796	-0.003	-11.062
Time Since Last T/A	0.000	3.453	0.000	3.195	0.000	2.933
Month FE	Yes		Yes		Yes	
Plant FE	Yes		Yes		Yes	
Observations	11,448		9,299		4,402	
R^2	0.09		0.08		0.16	

An observation is a plant-month for 107 plants from January 2001 - August 2011. "Time Since Last T/A" measures the number of months since the plant last experienced a planned outage (or Turn-Around). Utilization rate measured at the refining district level.

Table 17: Distillate Price Effects of an Average Outage

Specification	Outage Type	Average PADD Capacity (BPD)	Average Outage (BPD)	Average Outage (%)	Coeff. Estimate	Predicted Price Effect (CPG)	95% C.I.
A	Atmospheric Distillation Unit	3,395,525	141,058	4.15%	0.327	1.36	(0.43, 2.28)
B	Planned		83,064	2.45%	0.419	1.74	(0.57, 2.91)
	Unplanned		58,006	1.71%	0.188	0.78	(-0.64, 2.20)
C	Catalytic Cracking Unit	1,151,442	62,782	5.45%	0.286	1.56	(-0.91, 4.03)
D	Planned		34,515	3.00%	0.178	0.97	(-2.23, 4.18)
	Unplanned		28,267	2.45%	0.449	2.45	(-1.52, 6.42)
E	By Unit (Planned+Unplanned)						
	Atmospheric Distillation	3,395,525	141,058	4.15%	0.517	2.15	(0.89, 3.40)
	Catalytic Cracking	1,151,442	62,782	5.45%	-0.030	-0.16	(-3.06, 2.74)
	Catalytic Hydro Cracking	344,020	20,851	6.06%	-0.914	-5.54	(-14.88, 3.79)
	Reformer	684,763	35,992	5.26%	-1.706	-8.97	(-15.50, -2.43)
	Thermal Cracking	486,775	21,120	4.34%	1.623	7.04	(1.59, 12.50)

Regressions are run on data at the PADD-month level from January 2001 - December 2011. Prices are regressed on the crude oil price, the percent of the PADD's capacity that is offline, a hurricane indicator, gasoline stocks, and month, year, and PADD fixed effects. Separate regressions are run on each specification above (indicated in column 1).

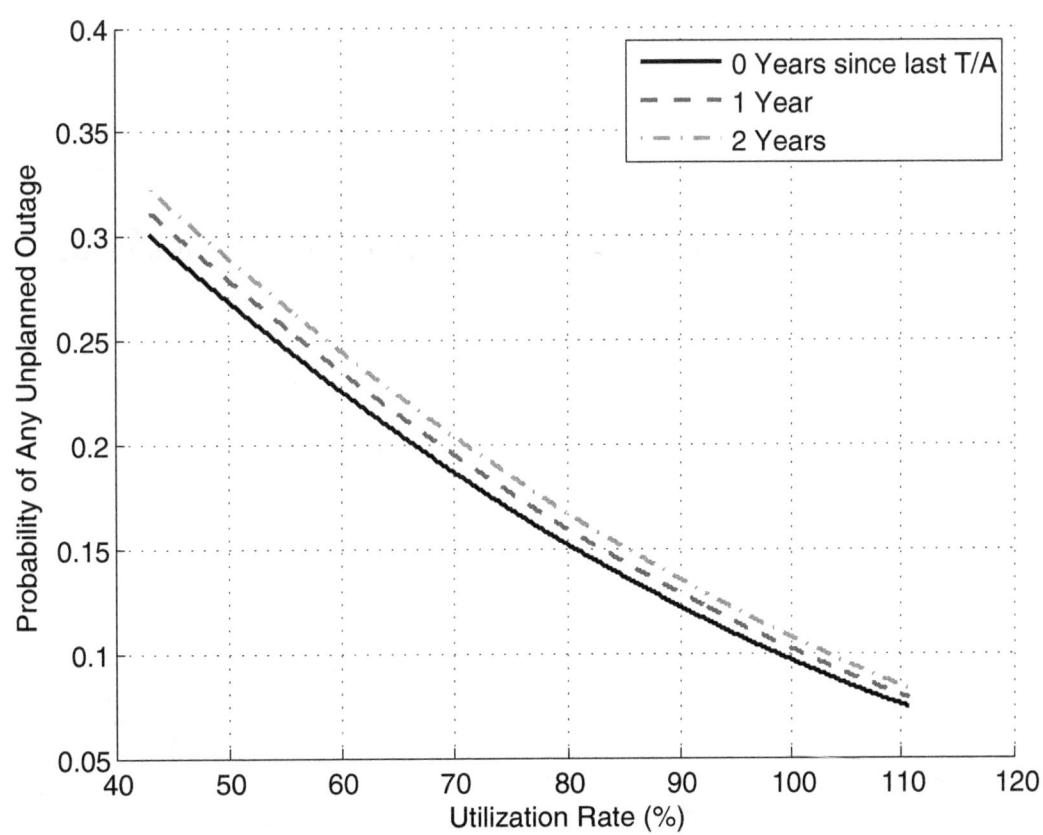

Figure 18: Probit Marginal Effects: Unplanned Outages by Utilization Rate

Figure 19: Effects of Outages on Distillate Prices by Utilization Rate

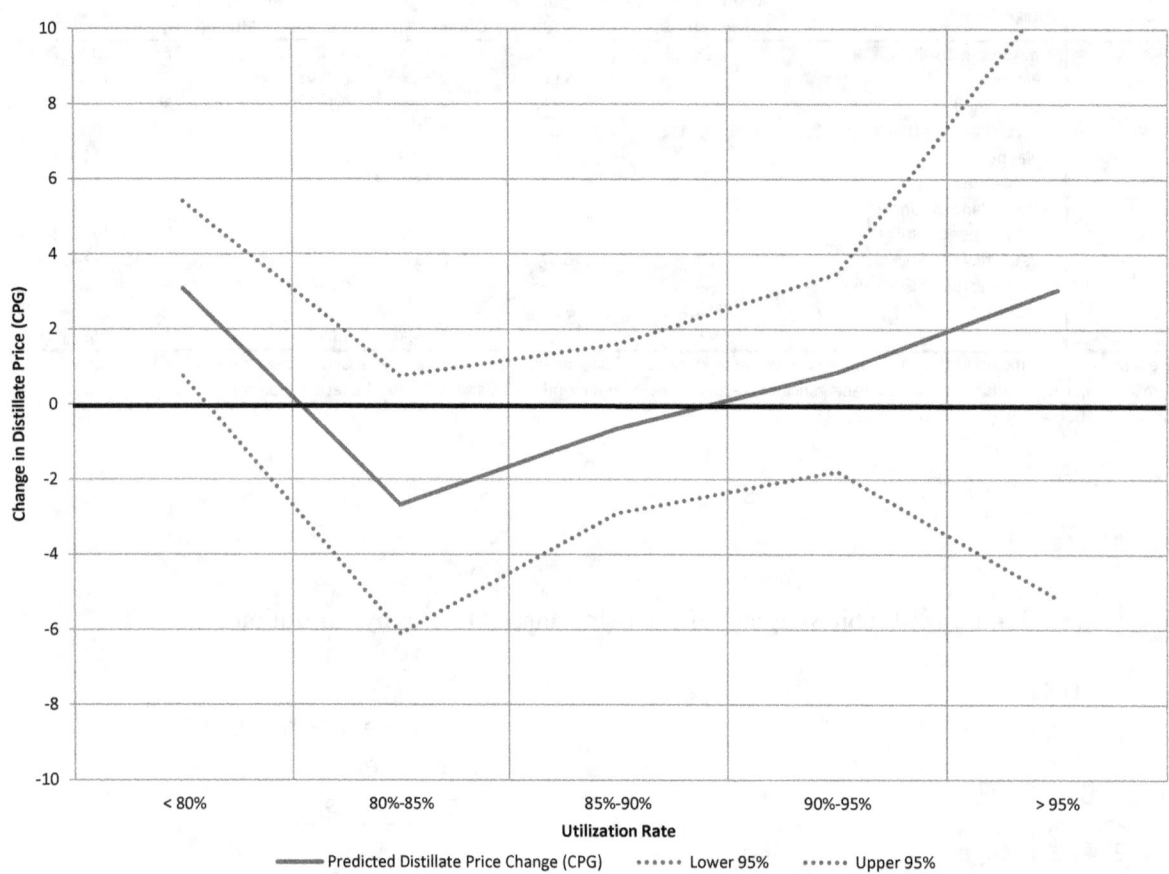

Predicted change in the distillate price from an average outage of atmospheric distillation capacity at different utilization rates.